Consuming Higher Education

ALSO AVAILABLE FROM BLOOMSBURY

Consuming Higher Education

Why Learning Can't be Bought

JOANNA WILLIAMS

B L O O M S B U R Y

LONDON • NEW DELHI • NEW YORK • SYDNEY

Bloomsbury Academic

An imprint of Bloomsbury Publishing Plc

50 Bedford Square
London
WC1B 3DP
UK

175 Fifth Avenue
New York
NY 10010
USA

www.bloomsbury.com

First published 2013

British Library Cataloguing-in-Publication Data

A catalogue record for this book is available from the British Library.

ISBN: HB: 978-1-4411-9450-3
PB: 978-1-4411-8360-6
PDF: 978-1-4411-6325-7
ePub: 978-1-4411-9337-7

Library of Congress Cataloging-in-Publication Data

A catalog record for this title is available from the Library of Congress.

Typeset by Fakenham Prepress Solutions, Fakenham, Norfolk NR21 8NN
Printed and bound in Great Britain

To Charlotte Williams

CONTENTS

FOREWORD

When was the last time a student said to you, "You have to pass me, I paid for it"? I have heard it before, more than once. Joanna Williams has heard it as well and she has a lot to say about what that sentiment can tell us about the state of higher education today.

This book's opening gambit, about a student demanding what some might term a 'return on investment', is meant to put into relief the changing relationships between university and students. When did higher education become another neo-liberal manifestation of the ideology of 'free' market enterprise? When did universities start describing students as clients? When did universities turn education into a commodity which they promote as a 'service'? When did 'education' become 'learning'? When did university presidents start providing annual reports as if they were chief financial officers reporting year-end stock values and price-earnings ratios? When did university-sponsored programmes offices start getting ever larger shares of externally funded research budgets committed to research in higher education? When did the goals of higher education become mostly about making students more employable? As Joanna Williams so piquantly asks in her piercing take on higher education today, when did students become consumers, and why?

With the major market metaphor of the title, *Consuming Higher Education*, Joanna Williams argues that 'student protestors, academics, politicians and commentators all appear to agree that higher education is essential for employability and is therefore a prerequisite for social mobility and social justice'. Why would employability and mobility be issues? Again, as Joanna Williams states, 'Given the paucity of intellectual purpose, students are perhaps left with few models with which to identify other than that of the consumer'. She goes on to claim that higher education in the UK and the USA has become disconnected from past purposes of seeking 'a moral or intellectual vision of truth, enlightenment, knowledge or under-standing'. Is her concern a last gasp of a declining liberal education tradition which has lost its grip on the institution as it lost its way in a free market world? I think not. Joanna Williams explains that the purpose of her book is to 'explore the many trends that come together to construct the student as consumer, and examine the impact consumer status has upon what it means to be a student today', and she hopes to reframe the purpose of higher education and its fundamental relationships of lecturer and student.

She writes: 'I argue for students to be considered as active participants in their education [...] to become the intellectual equals of their lecturers and make a contribution towards society's knowledge and understanding of the world'. Joanna Williams wants to re-envision the purposes of universities to go beyond what she describes as 'the narrowly individualistic pursuit of employability or socially instrumental goal of "inclusion".' Institutions of higher education were once considered providers of benefits to the public good. Have they now been engineered to provide for the employment needs of not only students as consumers but society as well?

Any effort to sort out the vagaries of the multiple purposes, past and present, of higher education is not nearly so clear-cut, as Joanna Williams well knows. She expends much effort in her book presenting and analysing the complexly nuanced circumstances of higher education in the UK and the USA today in order to demonstrate and detail the current trends producing marketised and consumerised higher education systems. She presents a brief but thorough account of the history of higher education in the UK and the USA. In doing so, she outlines the theological and spiritual origins of higher education whose varied purposes change through the centuries to accommodate multiple traditions, from conserving the wisdom of the past, to the development of 'modern' notions of rationality, to producing scientific knowledge, to the arrival of the public 'red-brick' (in the UK) and 'land-grant' (in the USA) institutions. From these origins she then looks at how the student-as-consumer is constructed today in the university as well as in society more generally and how that model of the consumer is taught to and learned by students. To elaborate upon that construction and how such education works, Joanna Williams examines the experience of students in higher education today, their attitudes towards learning, and their changing perceptions of what it means to be a student, particularly in terms of the impact of their experiences on the sense of self-identity that students develop. She also devotes a chapter to whether students' experience in higher education is 'empowering or infantilising'. Her final chapter ponders what universities might look like if students were not consumers, in order to propose a 'community of scholars', including faculty and students, to find a way through 'the perceived link between fee-paying and consumption, and find ways of financing an education worth wanting'.

If you have been discouraged by what you think may well be undesirable trends in higher education, I urge you to read this book – and to consider the questions Joanna Williams raises. If we are to alter the depiction of higher education today offered in this book, we need to change the way we understand what the university has become.

Arthur L. Wilson
Professor of Adult Education, Cornell University, USA

ACKNOWLEDGEMENTS

There are many people I need to thank for helping me to write this book. Jim Butcher has encouraged and supported me throughout the writing process, providing intellectual inspiration, critical feedback and numerous examples. I am most grateful to my students and colleagues at the University of Kent. I owe special thanks to Janice Malcolm and Fran Beaton for allowing me the academic freedom and time to pursue my own ideas. They have created a research environment which has helped me shape my arguments, despite the fact that they may not agree with all I write. In today's often fevered research environment I am fortunate indeed to have such colleagues. I need to thank Camille Nedelec-Lucas for references relating to universities in the United States. Above all, I owe a huge debt of gratitude to my friend and colleague Jennie Bristow whose impact upon this book cannot be underestimated. Jennie's intellectual generosity, vast knowledge, and political insight, combined with her ability to transform the most clumsily constructed sentences into readable prose, really helped to make this book a reality. It remains, of course, the case that all errors are mine alone. This book is dedicated to my children: George, Harry and Florence, as well as to my nieces and nephews, in the hope that in the future they will each find university to be worthy of their potential and their aspirations.

Introduction: It's not about the money

What it means to be a student in the UK appears to have changed radically within the space of a generation. When I began my time as an undergraduate at the University of Birmingham in 1992, I had no concept of a 'tuition fee'. University, it seemed to me, was much like school but on a bigger, more important, more intellectually challenging, more exciting scale. I was a student, not the recipient of a 'student experience', and it would never have occurred to me to complain about my university or even to ask myself whether I was 'satisfied'. As well as not having to worry about tuition costs, I also received a maintenance grant which covered most of my living expenses. A policy change implemented in 1992 meant that, each subsequent year, more of this grant was replaced by a loan, and I joined student demonstrators shouting to anyone who cared to listen that we would not repay our loans. But at the age of nineteen, the future seemed an awfully long way off. I did not draw a connection between loans and future debt; I did not see my time at university as inevitably leading to employment at all; and I was a stranger to the concept of 'social mobility'. I chose to study English Literature simply because it interested me.

It is easy to get the impression, from media commentators and politicians, that today's students are very different from those of previous generations. 'Students prefer studying to socialising,' states one newspaper headline (Frean, 2008), while another contradicts: 'UK students are the "least hard-working in Europe"'(Doughty, 2007). Today's students expect comfort way beyond the cheap shared rooms of yesteryear. The Vice-Chancellor of St Andrew's University in Scotland reports: 'Students are more demanding. Not only do they expect a single room, it has to be en-suite, have a TV in it and be cleaned for them.' He continues: 'This spreads into their learning experience – they expect essays to be marked clearly and back within a certain number of days, and to see their tutor regularly' (Woolcock and Malvern, 2008). Students are reported as making frequent complaints about their lecturers and universities if the service they receive does not meet expectations: student complaints are reported to have risen 37 per cent in the two years between 2008 and 2010 (Shepherd and Williams,

2010) and journalists are quick to suggest that the official number of complaints is likely to provide only a small indication of the real number of dissatisfied students.[1] Lecturers are complaining, too. 'The principles of the market and its managers more and more deeply suffuse the practices of education,' writes one frustrated academic, continuing: 'we have handed over meaning to the gangsters of propaganda and their hirelings in advertising' (Inglis, 2011).

Concerns about the workings of the academy are not restricted to higher education (HE) circles, but are increasingly splashed across the mainstream press – as are earnest debates about the identity of university students, once the preserve of introspective conversations in smoke-filled university bars. As the student population has expanded, both in numbers and in its diversity, students are often perceived as representatives of the younger generation as a whole, and the image presented of these young people can reveal much about society's attitudes towards and anxieties about the future. On both sides of the Atlantic, the media conducts a pervasive sense of uncertainty about the higher education sector. Questions about who should go to university, who should pay, and exactly how much, are all topics now discussed regularly in public. On the other hand, questions about why students should go to university at all are rarely asked.

The birth of the student consumer

One important reason for the growth in public discussion about HE in general and students in particular is the advent of university tuition fees directly paid by students. In Britain, the 2011 policy document, *Students at the Heart of the System*, produced by the Conservative and Liberal Democrat (Con-Lib) coalition government, legislated to allow Higher Education Institutions (HEIs) to set tuition fees at a level of up to £9,000 per academic year. In the USA, students have long been accustomed to paying at least a proportion of tuition fees; but over the past decade they have been faced with soaring costs, with Americans typically paying $45,000 for a four-year degree and $88,000 on average at a private university (Brzezinski, 2010). It is the payment of fees that provides the common-sense basis for the label, 'students as consumers', which has been employed since around 1965 in the USA[2] and 1995 in the UK.[3]

In the popular imagination, the British student consumer was officially born in July 1997 when the report of the National Committee of Inquiry into Higher Education (more popularly known as *The Dearing Report*) recommended that students make a flat-rate contribution towards the cost of their university tuition fees. The recent increases in tuition fees have led to debate about the status of students – 'Are They Students or Customers?', asks one *New York Times* blog[4] – and enhanced the perception that students are consumers of an increasingly marketised university system. One leading broadsheet newspaper in the UK made two references to students as consumers in 1998; this rose to 442 references in 2011.[5] That students should become consumers as a result of paying university tuition fees is often presented as an inevitable process. 'It is a hardly surprising consequence of the introduction of tuition fees that students – not to mention their parents, who are frequently the ones laying out some of the money – increasingly see themselves as consumers,' writes the editor of *The Guardian University Guide* (Wignall, 2007). With a similar assumption of common sense, it is noted in a different newspaper that: 'We are becoming a service society, and students increasingly think they are buying a service – for which they want a return' (Woolcock and Malvern, 2008).

Media representations of students reflect back to society some of the dominant ways in which what it means to be a student is understood today. This may also help to reconstruct ways of being a student for new generations. By assuming that consumer status is a *consequence* of tuition fees, journalists are both constructing and representing the student-consumer. One aim of this book is to interrogate the assumption that fee-paying necessarily leads students to position themselves as consumers of higher education, and to ask what other factors also contribute to the construction of the consumer model of HE.

The emergence of the student-consumer is often presented in the popular media as a generally positive social development, through which students are empowered to influence their experience of university. 'Consumer rights' are welcomed as allowing students 'more choice over where they study' and enabling them to 'get their money's worth' from universities charging tuition fees (Vasager and Shepherd, 2011). Newspapers report positively the fact that universities are now forced to seriously consider students' demands, thus: 'Two months after Sussex students made a submission to the university management, their institution responded with a 64-page document addressing their concerns' (Wignall, 2007). Students are encouraged to hold universities to account. The former President of the UK National Union of Students (NUS), Aaron Porter, argues: 'Universities must be better at dealing with complaints if they are to have any hope of students not feeling that they are being asked to pay more for less' (Sugden, 2011).

That universities should respond to student demands in this way implies that they will be competing for 'customers' (and importantly, their tuition fees) in a market-driven HE sector. It is this 'market' that the British government, self-consciously critical of the 'closed club of universities', wants to see implemented; ministers hope growing competition will lead both to greater financial efficiency and to the quality of HE being forced upwards (Grimston, 2011). Yet the fact that some commentators need to urge students and their parents to make the market 'work' ('to go beyond long-held visions of prestige, created by a parent's idea of a "proper" university' [Leach, 2006]) suggests that a market does not automatically arise because tuition fees are charged. Certainly it appears to be the case that tuition fees do little to deter potential students; in 2010, 42 per cent of American 25–35 year-olds paid large sums of money in order to obtain a graduate degree, compared to 38 per cent for the same British cohort who would have paid only a token amount (Brzezinski, 2010).

The public image of student-consumers choosing from within a HE marketplace shifts the commonly held perception of the purpose of the university. In contrast to an ivory tower of elite knowledge and earnest study, HE is presented as a financial investment for which students seek 'value for money'. Again, this soon assumes the status of common sense; universities 'spend increasing amounts on marketing to an increasingly money-fixated market of students who want value for money for their £3,000 per year' (Leach, 2006). Yet there is little discussion about what 'value for money' means in the context of education. It is most often linked to post-graduation employment prospects: 'What we are saying is that nowadays students, of course, are going to be thinking very carefully about the quality of the academic experience at university [...] what their job prospects are after they have been to university,' according to UK Universities Minister David Willetts (quoted in Sugden, 2011). Despite being presented as 'an expensive investment for which they can and should pay' (Brzezinski, 2010), however, there is clearly some anxiety about exactly how much a degree is worth to students: 'Graduating no longer guarantees a top job and a lot more pay' (MacErlean, 2005).

The recent increases in university tuition fees found on both sides of the Atlantic have, not surprisingly, been unpopular with students and there have been widely reported protests as a result. At my own institution, the University of Kent, a small group of protesters occupied a university building over the entire winter vacation of 2010/11 and only left due to the threat of a legal injunction. Nationally, many students marched through London in November 2010 to demonstrate their anger at increased fees. The media was uncertain what to make of these protesters; they were seen as either representing a new dawn of political radicalism and social conscience,[6] or as middle-class kids throwing tantrums over being forced to confront the real world.[7] In America too, anger at federal budget cuts to education spilled over into nationwide protests in March and April 2011.[8] There is also confusion in the American media; student debt is seen as either a stressful burden upon young adults or a sound personal investment (Hess, 2011).

Yet despite the contradictions and uncertainties surrounding current debates about students and universities, there are some surprising points of agreement. Student protesters, academics, politicians and commentators all appear to agree that HE is essential for employability and is therefore a prerequisite for social mobility and social justice. Such social and economic goals mean that education is far less likely nowadays to be linked to a moral or intellectual vision of truth, enlightenment, knowledge or understanding. Given the paucity of intellectual purpose, students are perhaps left with few models with which to identify other than that of the consumer.

This book will explore the many trends that come together to construct the student as consumer, and examine the impact consumer status has upon what it means to be a student today. Through this, the bigger question as to the purpose of higher education can be approached. I argue for students to be considered as active participants in their education, who have the potential to become the intellectual equals of their lecturers and make a contribution towards society's knowledge and understanding of the world. This necessitates a vision of the university that goes beyond the narrowly individualistic pursuit of employability or the socially instrumental goal of 'inclusion'.

Although this book is predominantly focused upon an analysis of recent changes that have taken place within British – and more specifically still, English – universities, I will also consider the development of the HE sector in the USA. Scotland, Northern Ireland and Wales have different funding arrangements for university students, although the fact that many of the trends identified in this book are also to be found in the HE sectors of these countries too suggests current changes in HE result from more than just financial arrangements. Throughout this book I explore the presentation of students and universities in policy documents, academic literature, and newspaper reports, and draw upon interviews I have conducted with students and policymakers.[9] Highlighting geographical and historical comparisons between and within two contrasting HE sectors may reveal both in a more subtle and contradictory perspective to that which tends to dominate the mainstream press. For example, from a British perspective, American universities are often lauded as the best in the world;[10] however, some UK academics and commentators demonstrate a sense of moral superiority towards what they perceive as an overly marketised system derided as having a 'Wal-Mart ethos' (Marcus, 2011). American commentators write with incredulity at British youngsters 'rioting' over the prospect of a mere £9,000 per year payment (Palmer, 2011), yet urge their European counterparts to 'avoid our higher education mistakes' (Ashley, 2011).

Between these polarised positions is a desire exhibited by successive UK governments to follow the HE system of the USA. The drive among politicians to emulate the American HE sector has been blamed by some academics for the creeping marketisation and commercialisation of HE, as well as the emergence of the student as consumer on British soil. This book will explore what exactly British politicians consider so worthy of imitation in the US system, and question the accuracy of the image that British politicians hold and promote of American universities. Often it seems that changes are set in place to replicate an image of the US HE sector that may exist only in the imagination of a few politicians and their advisors.

Fee-paying and the consumption of education

At its simplest, the concept of the student as consumer is associated with someone who, as a result of financial exchange, considers themselves to have purchased, and is therefore entitled to possess, a particular product (a degree) or to expect access to a certain level of service (staff and resources). There is an assumption that the student consumer 'will want to see obvious, tangible benefits from their studies, whether in terms of an inherently valuable qualification or as a route to a particular form of employment' (Kaye, Bickel and Birtwistle, 2006: 86). The British academic A. C. Grayling describes a direct connection between fee-paying and the development of behaviour and attitudes associated with customers: 'If students or students' parents are personally paying more for higher education, they will in effect become consumers, and what they are purchasing – a degree – will become a commodity. In the rest of the commercial world the consumer is right and what he demands is what the retailer must supply' (Grayling, 2002).

Paying fees has certainly had an impact upon the way students relate to their lecturers, learning and universities. However, Grayling's view suggests it is fee-paying alone that transforms students into customers, and that students did not act as consumers before the introduction of tuition fees. I will argue that this is not the case and that tuition fees are as much a symptom as a cause of the political transformation of HE and what it means to be a student. It is possible for students to adopt the attitudes and behaviour of a consumer without paying fees; similarly, fee-paying need not contradict a commitment to intellectual engagement. Rather, a number of social, political and cultural trends come together to produce the student consumer.

In many ways, the identification of the 'student as consumer' in the UK media at the time students first began to pay tuition fees merely put a name to an existing trend. The cultural shift in how students consider themselves in relation to their studies and how they are perceived by others in society had already begun to take place. Students are constructed as consumers through the media, institutional policies, government ministers, schools, careers advisers, and their peers and parents. Even before the introduction of tuition fees directly paid by students, potential entrants to HE were often encouraged by teachers, parents and university marketing departments to seek out the best 'product'. This was most likely based upon a perception of the historical status or reputation of the institution or simply the university that appeared to perform most successfully based on league table rankings which appear in newspapers.

Historically, even in the UK, the concept of paying for education is not new. Education, in the form of instruction, has long been purchasable by wealthy individuals and families. The free access to state-funded universities and generous student grants enjoyed by many in the UK fortunate enough to gain a place at university in the latter half of the twentieth century was an historical anomaly. Yet in previous eras, the act of purchase did not automatically engender the consumerist attitudes and behaviour, such as expecting to achieve certain grades as a result of payment and attendance, found in some of today's students. This seems to have developed separately. For example in 2003, five years after students first made a contribution to the cost of their university tuition, a legal case recognised the right of students to be treated like consumers and financially compensated if their expectations as to the level of service received were not met.[11] This implies that the payment of a contribution towards the cost of tuition fees did not, *per se*, enshrine consumer status: a separate court judgement was needed for this to be the case.

For consistency, throughout this book I shall refer to debates around 'students as consumers' rather than 'customers'. However, often the terms 'consumer' and 'customer' are used interchangeably in everyday discourse to describe fee-paying students. For example, Ian Pearson, then Labour Member of Parliament (MP) for Dudley South in the UK, argued in 2000: 'It is good for the system that students exert their consumer rights [...] I want to see students empowered as customers.'[12] Here students are presented as consumers and customers at the same time. We also see that the labelling of students as consumers begins to imply more than just fee-paying but also ways of feeling (*empowered*) and behaving (*exerting rights*).

The words 'consumer' and 'customer' arguably have subtly different meanings: dictionary definitions suggest a consumer can be defined as one who *uses* a commodity or services whilst a customer *purchases* goods or services. British Professor of Higher Education Ron Barnett suggests: 'A consumer is one who consumes the service extended to him or her. A customer, on the other hand, extends his or her custom to the provider ... in other words the customer has a greater influence in a market relationship than the consumer' (Barnett, 2011: 43).

When used to describe students, the terms 'customer' and 'consumer' rarely describe a literal transactional relationship. In the UK, fee-paying students do not pay per lecture or seminar; indeed, most never make any financial transaction at all, as this is made on their behalf by the Student Loans Company (SLC) and they merely receive a letter informing them that their fees have been paid. Rather, the terms are used metaphorically to describe an *attitude* adopted by some students. This attitude, or sensibility, is defined less by the act of purchase and far more by the expectations and sense of entitlement that students increasingly demonstrate in relation to HE. These consumer attitudes have developed irrespective of the charging of tuition fees. Put simply, if university tuition fees were ended tomorrow, the assumptions that educational success is a right irrespective of intellectual endeavour, and that the purpose of a degree is to make people employable, would remain.

That students should act and behave as if entitled to an education in the form of a product is presented both positively and negatively in public debate. For example, the large increase in the number of students lodging formal complaints that has been noted by the Office of the Independent Adjudicator (OIA)[13] is interpreted as both good and bad for the HE sector. While some decry the fact that 'Students are not as easygoing as they might be, it seems, and are complaining about everything from exam papers to the price of a college cappuccino'[14], others are keen to see 'students empowered as customers' who 'complain if they feel they're not getting the quality of teaching and other services that they deserve.'[15]

The use of the word 'empowered' implies that students lacked 'power' when they did not pay fees. This certainly seems to be the belief of British government ministers and their policy advisers, who have described the creation of a HE market as 'a surer way to drive up quality than any attempt at central planning.'[16] In other words, it is argued that the operation of consumer choice within a marketised HE sector will drive up standards, and therefore the student as consumer is a positive force: the 'good' student will exercise consumer choice and 'drive up the quality' of HE for others. Such assumptions may suggest that HE is at times perceived as a commodity designed to be packaged and consumed, and that it has an inherent financial value which can, once purchased, be traded in the post-graduation labour market.

The adoption by critical commentators within and without the academy of the phrase 'students as consumers' suggests something about the cultural assumptions society holds of today's students: that they seek passive possession of a degree commodity rather than active intellectual engagement in the learning process; that they expect to receive a service commensurate with the fees paid; that they will seek legal or financial redress if their expectations are not met. A number of academics have critiqued the emergence of the student consumer, encapsulated in Grayling's colourful declaration that 'I'm not a commodity'.[17] The American academic Paul Trout wrote in 1997 that 'Students who think of themselves as customers study only when it is convenient (like shopping), expect satisfaction regardless of effort [...] and assume that academic success, including graduation, is guaranteed' (Trout, 1997: 50). Yet such assumptions may expose a degree of condescension and prejudice towards younger generations and a myth of a 'golden age' in HE.

Today, as ever, students cannot be treated as a homogenous group; not all students will consider themselves to be consumers. As this book explores, there are many forces encouraging students to adopt consumer attitudes, not least the behaviour of lecturers and universities themselves. Such socialisation leads many students to believe that behaving as a consumer is what is expected of them. The fact that, even today, not all students consider themselves to be consumers further suggests that there is not a simple correlation between paying fees and the adoption of consumer attitudes. It is possible for the payment of tuition fees to occur without students being transformed into consumers. Indeed, Grayling notes that in different social and political periods, payment may have 'the effect not of commodifying their learning, but galvanising their endeavours on their own behalf' (Grayling, 2002).

The converse is also true; in a marketised HE sector it is entirely plausible that students may act as consumers without paying tuition fees (Becher and Trowler, 2001: 8). British academics Mike Molesworth, Elizabeth Nixon and Richard Scullion have identified a shift in focus from 'being' a student to 'having' a degree, which pre-dates direct payment of tuition fees (Molesworth, Nixon and Scullion, 2009). Indeed, students may be encouraged to act in this way through various educational initiatives such as student satisfaction surveys, or modularised courses that package knowledge according to learning outcomes. Once constructed, the consumer identity demands a response: while some students may consciously reject customer status as demeaning their intellectual endeavours, others may welcome it as helping to raise the quality and quantity of tuition.

That the payment of fees is not so central to the student-as-consumer is (perhaps somewhat ironically) evident in the anti-fees protests that took place in the UK in the final months of 2010. The government's decision to accept formally many of the proposals made in Lord Browne's Review of University Finance, *Securing a Sustainable Future for Higher Education* (more popularly known as *The Browne Review*), published in November 2010, was met by large and at times violent opposition from student protesters. Such demonstrations could be interpreted as indicating students' rejection of the assumption that they are customers. Indeed for some students this was indeed the case. However, indicating one's unhappiness with fee-paying is not always the same as rejecting consumerist attitudes. Indeed, the opposite may be the case, and unhappiness with the level of fees may actually represent the mainstream adoption of a consumerist attitude. Many protesters argued that HE, as a prerequisite for employability and social mobility, was a 'right', and that in making students pay more money they were being denied this entitlement. When presented in this way, HE is still perceived of as an investment product – it is just demanded that the product be made available to more of the population, at a cheaper price or better quality.

Similarly, the Browne Review, although going further than any previous review of HE funding in recommending the marketisation of the sector, makes no direct reference to students as either customers or consumers. Browne's suggestions to empower students and promote employability often chime with protesters' concerns. At times, the only real point of disagreement between protesters and government ministers appears to be who should pick up the bill for a university place.

Debating the market: HE as metaphor

Many students today express distaste at being seen as consumers of anything. Anti-capitalist protests have gained momentum, and markets in any form are seen to represent an acquisitive form of capitalism. In such a context, HE markets become a focus for all that is seen as politically objectionable: corporate profiteering, social inequality and big business. Education becomes merely one more marketised 'neo-liberal' commodity to object to among many. Yet such negative critiques of the market, directed at banks and universities alike, do little to articulate what is special about education. Universities are portrayed as simply another example of capitalist greed, and education another over-priced commodity.

One view holds that markets 'corrupt children, infantilise adults and swallow citizens whole' (Barber, 2008) and an image is presented of universities and lecturers as out to manipulate vulnerable young students. In 2011 the US government sued the company Education Management Corporation on the grounds that it had a 'boiler-room style sales culture': 'Its recruiters used high-pressure sales techniques, and inflated claims about career placement to increase student enrolment, regardless of applicants' qualifications' (Nocera, 2011). The assumption here is that students would be persuaded to sign up for a programme of study they were not interested in, at an institution they did not wish to attend, simply because of pressurised sales techniques. Such a view risks infantilising students on the one hand and on the other demonising private companies when universities themselves can employ aggressive sales techniques and government information leaflets can create the impression that attending higher education is the only worthwhile option for school-leavers.

In treating students as consumers needing to be satisfied, universities can play a role in infantilising students through reducing intellectual challenge to the completion of modules and replacing academic relationships with customer care contracts. Students themselves do not always challenge such infantilisation. Protesters involved in the University of Kent's occupation in December 2010 and January 2011 against the increase in tuition fees complained that the university was not fulfilling its duty of care towards them. Instead of demanding to be listened to as independent, autonomous adults, protesters were, in effect, asking to be better looked after.

One reason why education is not a commodity like any other is that its inherent worth varies with each individual who shares the same surface experience, depending upon the extent of the student's engagement, motivation and prior learning. Therefore value judgements as to the worth of education cannot be made in advance of engagement in learning processes. For this reason, HE has been described as a 'post-experience good' (Weimer and Vining, 1992), 'the quality of which can only be appreciated after, indeed long after it has been experienced' (Brown, 2010). Yet despite the difficulty in assessing the value of education as a commodity, it is unfair to decry students as irrational consumers in need of protection from a red-toothed HE market. In selecting a university, students try to explore a range of seemingly rational mechanisms to enable them to make best sense of their choice, such as drawing upon the advice of friends and family members, and assessing information in the public domain. If students are not considered old or wise enough to make sensible decisions about where they study, serious questions surely need to be asked about whether they are old or wise enough to go to university at all.

Academic debate surrounding HE on both sides of the Atlantic raises concerns about the increased marketisation and commercialisation taking place within the sector through 'a broader policy shift away from the Keynesian welfare state settlement towards a new settlement based on neo-liberalism which introduced mechanisms of the market and new managerialism into higher education' (Naidoo and Jamieson, 2005: 270). Marketisation has been defined as the political, ideological and economic processes through which institutions are forced 'to compete against one another for resources and funding', following the 'managerial models of private and especially public sector corporations' (Furedi, 2011: 1). Commercialisation, on the other hand, is used to refer to 'efforts within the university to make a profit from teaching, research and other campus activities' (Bok, 2003: 3). Similarly, the label 'academic capitalism' has been used to criticise HE sectors in which decisions are 'driven by market forces' and 'faculty and professional staff expend their human capital stocks increasingly in competitive situations' as 'state-subsidized entrepreneurs' (Slaughter and Leslie, 1997: 9). Others write of higher education as having been 'de-churched' – that is, having had its 'ideological justification recast in terms of corporatization and commodification' and in so doing, having 'become subject to serious state surveillance' (Tuchman, 2009: 41). It is the coming together of these trends that causes the construction of students as consumers – an outcome which, in turn, exacerbates the trends further.

In public debate, the terms 'marketisation' and 'commercialisation' are often used interchangeably. For the purposes of this book, I define 'marketisation' primarily as the process by which institutions compete for customers – and a market in HE potentially occurs as soon as there is more than one university bidding to attract students. This could suggest the presence of some very primitive form of HE market going back hundreds of years and pre-dating any concept of students as consumers (Furedi, 2011; Evans, 2004). As we will explore in the following chapter, however, other factors need to be present for marketisation to become a reality. Universities need to have plentiful affordable residential accommodation, or there needs to be efficient national transport links to make a national, or even international, marketplace for students possible. In addition, a proportion of university funding needs to follow individual students to force universities to compete over recruitment.

There is a sense among commentators within and without the academy that the marketisation of HE has intensified over the past decade.[18] Indeed, some have lauded this development as a positive force for raising standards. For example, the Browne Review suggests that the creation of a market, and active competition between institutions within the HE sector, will drive up the quality of the student experience and improve provision across the whole sector (Browne, 2010: 8). While the veracity of this claim is highly contestable,[19] it appears to be accepted as common sense by politicians and government advisors.[20]

Critics argue that the logic of market forces applied to HE serves to lower educational standards, as universities seek to promote themselves to students on the basis of high pass marks and a generous likelihood of achieving top marks. British Professor of HE Policy Roger Brown argues that markets 'encourage an academic "arms race" for prestige amongst all institutions, which rapidly increases the costs of higher education and devalues the improvement of student learning.' Furthermore, he points out, 'the rising financial costs of higher education are not matched by equivalent social benefits' (Brown, 2011: 48). Brown suggests such competition removes any social focus from the role of universities: marketisation 'threatens the "contract" that higher education has with society whereby universities enjoy various privileges (such as academic autonomy and financial subsidies from government) in return for producing public goods (such as a well educated labour force or scientific and technological advancements) which would not otherwise be available.'[21]

American academics Sheila Slaughter and Larry Leslie likewise argue that: 'Professionals negotiated a tacit social contract with the community at large, in which they received monopolies of practice in return for disinterestedly serving the public good' (Slaughter and Leslie, 1997: 4). Stefan Collini, Professor of English from the University of Cambridge, argues that marketisation means it will be left to student choice to determine 'what and how universities teach, and indeed in some cases whether they exist at all' (Collini, 2010). Other critics argue that marketisation leads to a homogenisation within the HE sector as institutions seek to make themselves distinctive to customers, but not so distinct as to be outside of the market altogether. This acknowledges that students can be conservative in their choices and are not always prepared to gamble with what they may consider to be their future career prospects.[22]

The market-driven competition among institutions for income from students, businesses and research grants puts an emphasis upon prestige and reputation. 'Branding', reputation management and the perception of quality become arguably more important than the reality of what happens in a university. Money coming into the universities may be directed away from teaching and research and towards marketing departments. Branding universities has certainly become a major exercise with 'conspicuous expenditure on things like [...] marketing, recruitment, student residences, athletics facilities' (Brown, 2010). In the UK, the former Thames Valley University is hoping that a name change to the University of West London will enable a rebranding of the public image of the institution (Morgan, 2011). One problem with perceived reputation, quantified in league table positions, is that education is at best a 'positional market where what counts is relative position' (Hirsch, 1976, cited in Brown, op. cit.). No matter how good a university actually is, all that counts in terms of the marketplace is only how good it is *perceived to be.*

League tables are both a cause and an effect of increased marketisation. Universities focus upon student satisfaction, perhaps at the expense of intellectual struggle, in order to secure high positions in the league tables. Lecturers may lose their right to academic freedom, or at least find the right more difficult to exercise,[23] if universities want to maintain a tighter grip on the public image of the institution. One lecturer reports on a meeting with 'image consultants' prior to a university open day for new students: 'We were given advice on which words to use, what not to say and how to answer difficult questions. We also have to scrub up and take fashion advice so we all look presentable.'[24]

Despite this criticism of the HE market, there is also some acknowledgement that what we have in reality, especially in the UK, is not a genuine 'free' market but instead a 'pseudo-market' that is heavily supported and regulated by the state (Furedi, 2011; Brown, 2011). As an example, British universities are neither free to charge whatever the market will support nor to attract as many students as they feel able. In addition, universities are accountable to government for a number of key areas of their institutional decision-making. Such a pseudo-market has been in existence since long before students were first labelled as consumers.

Many academics are also critical of the commercialisation of universities. I define 'commercialisation' as the money-making, business face of the university. This is not necessarily making money for profit alone; it may involve generating income from one part of the university to subsidise less financially lucrative departments elsewhere in the institution. This may include selling products ranging from branded goods to accommodation directly to students as customers of the university. Commercialisation also refers to other ways in which universities make money, such as selling services to business; seeking sponsorship from business for particular departments, sporting activities or even lectureships; renting campus space to businesses so that student common rooms, for example, may become taken over by brand-name coffee shops; or simply renting campus space to advertisers. Significantly, commercialisation increasingly refers to selling the 'core product' of the university: that is, education. This selling of education as a product, or a commodity, is not especially new. The former Principal of Yale University, Derek Bok, points to the growth in adult education in the USA after the Second World War, when universities sought to make money through offering continuing education to professionals who felt the need to acquire new skills and knowledge in an increasingly complex society (Bok, 2003: 12). However, the process of selling education has become much more widespread and standardised in recent decades, and one aim of this book is to draw out what is distinct and significant about the commercialisation processes at work today.

The idea that universities are becoming transformed into commercial enterprises with students as their customers provokes significant distaste, particularly among critics who consider themselves left-wing; as does the fear that students are exploited as a campus-bound captive audience for big business. It has been suggested that, for some ideologically driven critics, arguing against the commercialisation of HE has become a 'stand-in' for more general resistance to neo-liberal capitalism (Scullion, Molesworth and Nixon, 2011: 228). However, just as with marketisation, it is not the presence of commercial activity alone that transforms students into consumers of education. Many market-savvy youngsters are comfortable with negotiating commercial activity on campus and find it perfectly plausible that one could engage in a commercial contract when purchasing food, books or accommodation, yet approach education, subject knowledge and learning in a different way.

Consuming Higher Education argues that it is neither the payment of tuition fees, nor the presence of commercial activity at a university which markets itself in competition with other institutions, that automatically leads to the corruption of education or the wholesale transformation of students into consumers. Rather, understanding this troubling process requires a deeper examination of the historical development of the university sector, and an interrogation of the contemporary social, political and cultural trends which help transform students into consumers. From this we can hope to gain a sober assessment of the impact this shift has had upon students' learning, and the mission of education and universities in general.

The first part of the book considers how the student consumer has come into being. Chapter 1 focuses specifically upon the historical development of HE in the USA and in the UK until the mid–1990s. An analysis of the key national policies in relation to the social, political and economic climate from which they emerged enables consideration of the perceived purpose of universities and the funding of HE. Chapter 2 looks at how the student consumer is constructed today, through a focus specifically upon the status of students within universities and how this is reflected in broader society. I consider student numbers; changes in the social composition of the university; and, perhaps most importantly, changes in how students finance their period of study. I also explore other factors that have influenced the construction of the student consumer, such as a government and institutional focus upon human capital, employability and social mobility (which has emerged strongly from universities in the USA). Chapter 3 looks at how students in both the UK and the USA are taught by institutions, school teachers and university lecturers to think of themselves as consumers.

The second half of this book explores the impact that being constructed as a consumer has upon the experience of being a student. Chapter 4 examines what consumer status means for students' attitudes to learning, knowledge and their relationship with lecturers. The metaphor of the student consumer is often extended by critical commentators to suggest that knowledge is now a commodity, and lecturers merely service providers. Chapter 5 analyses changing perceptions of what it means to be a student, and how this intersects with students' sense of self-identity. Chapter 6 discusses whether consumer status is experienced as empowering or infantilising by students. Finally, Chapter 7 asks how universities might look if students were not consumers, and explores the potential for alternative constructions of student identity to emerge within the confines of contemporary culture.

Some current research suggests that a proportion of undergraduate students reject the label of consumer (Williams, 2011a; Molesworth, Nixon and Scullion, 2009). Throughout this book I argue that many young people are genuinely excited by their subject choices and seek intellectual challenge from their time at university, and that universities and individual lecturers can do much to question the construction of the student as consumer. In making the case for quality education, with students and lecturers united as a community of scholars, it can be possible to break down the perceived link between fee-paying and consumption, and find ways of financing an education worth wanting.

Endnotes

1 Shepherd and Williams (15/06/10).

2 See, for example, Riesman (1980).

3 See, for example, Hill (1995).

4 http://roomfordebate.blogs.nytimes.com/2010/01/03/are-they-students-or-customers/? gwh=8D1AB71C984502BEC5836660BCEA71C0 [accessed 19/07/12].

5 *The Guardian*, see http://www.guardian.co.uk [accessed 19/07/12].

6 See, for example, Chessum (2010).

7 See, for example, Littlejohn (2010).

8 Al Arabiya News (02/07/11).

9 In-depth, semi-structured interviews were conducted with twenty first-year undergraduate students at universities in the south-east of England in January and February 2011.

10 University World League Table Rankings (7/10/11) *Times Higher Education*

11 As reported in *The Daily Telegraph* (4/03/03).

12 As reported in *The Independent* (11/05/00).

13 As reported in *The Guardian* (15/06/10).

14 As reported in *The Times* (23/08/05).

15 As reported in *The Independent* (11/05/00).

16 *Securing a Sustainable Future for Higher Education*, 'The Browne Report' (DBIS 2010).

17 As reported in *The Independent* (3/11/02). Other scholarly critiques of the status of students as consumers include work by Morley (2003); Kaye, Bickel and Birtwhistle (2006); Naidoo and Jamieson (2005).

18 See, for example, Morley (2003); Kaye, Bickel and Birtwhistle (2006); Molesworth, Nixon and Scullion (2009).

19 See, for example, Brown (2010); Tuchman (2009); Bok (2003).

20 See, for example, the 2011 White Paper, *Higher Education: Students at the Heart of the System*.

21 Brown (2011), 155.

22 See Tuchman (2009).

23 Williams, J. (2010) 'The student customer is not always right' in *Spiked Online*, http://www.spiked-online.com/index.php/site/article/9847/ [accessed 19/07/12].

24 Blogconfidential (17/03/11), *Times Higher Education*.

1

Students within a changing university

Students have not always been considered consumers of higher education. Nor did the student-as-consumer arrive in the UK merely as a result of the 2011 legislation that raised individual tuition fee payments, as much of the recent media debate might suggest. This chapter explores the HE landscape in the USA and the UK before the vocabulary of markets, consumer choice and student satisfaction replaced the language of knowledge, learning and education. From this historical background it becomes possible to trace the social, economic and political conditions that gave birth to the student as consumer. This chapter considers key government policies that have shaped the HE sectors in both the USA and the UK up to the mid–1990s.

Many debates recur throughout the history of HE, the chief of which is the purpose of universities. Rhetorical battles between supporters of vocational education and liberal education echo across the generations. Likewise, discussion as to who should go to university began in earnest from the middle of the nineteenth century. Neither of these debates has been resolved. Without understating the political and cultural pressures that operated around universities in the past, or naively assuming a 'golden age' of higher education, we can trace a general shift away from a more liberal notion of higher education being important for its own sake, towards a more instrumental connection to the employment prospects of individuals. Over more recent years, HE has moved from being broadly viewed as a public good of benefit to society, to a private good of benefit mainly to the individual student.

Today, policy makers argue that higher education should primarily serve an economic purpose in ensuring individual employability and international competitiveness; or a social purpose in creating an inclusive society where individual social mobility, and national social justice, can be seen to occur. Before passing judgement upon either of these positions it is important to note that both locate the purpose of a university as external to education. British sociologist Frank Furedi notes that 'an instrumental economic agenda has converged with an anti-elitist social engineering imperative, in a joint attack on academic, subject based education' (Furedi, 2009: 40). It is assumed today that education must indeed have a stated purpose; that it is not just important in and of itself.

Education, and higher education in particular, represents the historical accumulation of society's collective knowledge and understanding. The content, rather than the form, of higher education represents a nation's intellectual heritage: the knowledge, skills and traditions that are considered worth passing from one generation to the next. Hannah Arendt suggests it is because children are 'born into an already existing world' that educators have a particular responsibility to play a role in passing on society's knowledge, 'even though they may, secretly or openly, wish it were other than it is' (Arendt, 1954: 185–6). Through the passing on of this knowledge, 'individuals gain an understanding of themselves through familiarity with the unfolding of the human world' (Furedi, 2009: 47). It is for this reason that Michael Oakeshott refers to education as a 'conversation between the generations' (in Pring, 2004: 28).

Society's attitude towards the institutions and people that comprise the higher education sector in many ways represents the regard in which this national intellectual heritage is held. A need to locate the purpose of HE as external to learning for its own sake is perhaps indicative of a broader crisis in relation to the knowledge that is considered sufficiently important to pass from one generation to the next. If the intellectual elite in society are no longer able to confidently assert a body of knowledge that future citizens should be able to master, interpret, add to, and make their own, then universities necessarily fall back upon instrumental purposes to justify their existence. Arendt notes: 'the crisis of authority in education is most closely connected with the crisis of tradition, that is with the crisis in our attitude toward the realm of the past' (Arendt, 1954: 190). The emergence of the student-as-consumer then represents not just a financial or even a political shift within the HE sector, but fundamentally an educational shift too.

When students are no longer perceived to be potential contributors to the public intellectual capital of the nation, there are perhaps few alternatives to the student-as-private-investor model. The brief historical sweep of two major national HE sectors provided here aims to show how, by the mid–1990s, the student consumer had become an established feature of the US HE sector; and how, even before the introduction of tuition fees paid directly by students in the UK, the scene had been set for the emergence of the student-as-consumer here too.

A brief history of higher education in Britain and America

The history of universities in England dates back as far as 1096, when a centre of teaching and learning is recorded as existing in Oxford. This was to become the first university in the English-speaking world (Robinson, 2010: xii). The University of Cambridge followed a little over 100 years later, when a group of scholars banished from Oxford set up an alternative home. These universities were founded by the Catholic Church as essentially monastic institutions, designed for young men to spend time dedicated to theological study before entering the Priesthood. The founders of these institutions were influenced by the work of St Augustine and, going back even further, Plato's Academy, which aimed to keep men cloistered from the concerns of everyday life (in Carr, 2009: 5). Later years brought the founding of the 'Ancient Universities' in Scotland: institutions that developed during the Renaissance and Medieval periods, when King James II (1437–60) wanted Scottish universities to rival Oxford and Cambridge and established St Andrews (1413) and Glasgow University (1451).

These universities were exclusively religious institutions until the Reformation, when King Henry VIII ordered the dissolution of the Catholic Monasteries in 1534. One impact of the Reformation was to begin slowly to challenge the narrowly religious focus of universities. The reign of Queen Elizabeth I (1558–1603) marked the start of the Renaissance in England and the intellectual excitement of the era further served to loosen the religious grip on universities and broaden the range of subjects taught in them. By the middle of the seventeenth century John Locke graduated from Oxford University having studied medicine, 'natural philosophy' and philosophy (Smith, 2001: 45).

The first American universities had similar religious beginnings to those in Britain, but were founded by members of the Protestant faith rather than the Catholic Church. Harvard College was the first university to be established in 1636, followed by the College of William and Mary in Virginia in 1693, and the University of Pennsylvania in 1751. Despite religious affiliation, these privately funded institutions were proud to be free from the political control of the British colonial government (Heller, 2011: x).

For some students in the seventeenth and eighteenth centuries, entering university would have been a precursor to their becoming clergymen, their divinely determined 'vocation' in life. The purpose of a university could, then, perhaps be considered vocational, in the sense that it served as a form of training for a future life path. Today, as definitions of vocational education have shifted, we would probably consider the education received by students at this time as more broadly academic than narrowly practical. Indeed, it is only since 1987 that 'training' to join the Priesthood in Britain has moved away from a purely academic, philosophical and theological focus to include more practical aspects of delivering ministry.[1] For other students in the seventeenth and eighteenth centuries, links to the Church were more of a formality and did not prevent them from studying a broad-based range of subjects.

From the mid-seventeenth century until the end of the nineteenth century, the Enlightenment marked a final cultural departure from the Middle Ages. With the Enlightenment came the possibility of a rationalist, scientific understanding of the world achieved through independent scholarship. New fields of study emerged in areas such as mathematics, astronomy, physics, politics and economics. Other subjects such as philosophy and medicine were radically updated and expanded. Huge leaps in understanding were made and much new knowledge was discovered. More of the population than ever before sought to engage in intellectual pursuits. For the most part, these intellectual developments took place outside of the universities and only latterly had an impact upon the academy.

The development of education in America at this time was greatly influenced by the work of the British Enlightenment philosopher John Locke (1632–1704), who described the human mind as a 'tabula rasa' [blank slate] – a concept that implied that the mind could be perfected through the formative influence of education. This was considered revolutionary because up to this point it had been believed that knowledge, and especially moral sense, was innate or 'God-given', and that therefore education was of strictly limited use. The notion of humans as being perfectible through knowledge gave new impetus to schools and universities. In America, the demand for the building of more universities was driven by Independence in 1776; Locke's work had also been influential in the writing of the American Declaration of Independence. Citizens of an independent nation sought to determine their own intellectual future. In 1791 the Bill of Rights was passed by Congress, and education became a function of state rather than federal government. States then began to charter public universities to supplement the private, often church-funded institutions.

Only towards the end of the Enlightenment period did British universities come to be influenced by philosophies of what would now be termed 'liberal education': the promotion of learning for its own sake, to seek truth and to broaden knowledge as an end in itself, as opposed to serving a religious purpose. The liberal ideal is often considered to stand in opposition to education that has a vocational, practical utility. John Stewart Mill, in his 1867 *Inaugural Address to the University of St Andrews*, describes the role of a university as 'not a place of professional education', because he suggests subjects such as law and medicine are 'no part of what every generation owes the next as that on which its civilisation and worth will principally depend' (Mill, 1867). As with the Church Elders who founded the earliest universities, the Enlightenment proponents of liberal education were also influenced by Plato (427–347 BC) and his Academy, by the ideas of Socrates, and by the teachings of St Augustine (354–430 AD). Socrates and Plato instigated a liberal concept of education through their belief that wisdom was 'the chief of all virtues' and that 'the key goal of human enquiry is not the achievement of sensual satisfaction, wealth, status or even any more reputable or practical end – but the cultivation of that virtue which is its own end and reward' (in Carr, 2009: 2).

Towards the end of the Enlightenment, the work of German educational philosopher Wilhelm von Humboldt (1767–1835) had an impact on the founding principles of American and European universities, and British universities to a lesser extent. In the *Theory of Human Education* (circa 1793) Humboldt considered education in relation to the 'demands which must be made of a nation, of an age and of the human race'. He linked education to truth and virtue to better the 'concept of mankind' (in Hohendorf, 2000). Humboldt argued that the individual must 'absorb the great mass of material offered to him by the world around him and by his inner existence, using all the possibilities of his receptiveness; he must then reshape that material with all the energies of his own activity and appropriate it to himself so as to create an interaction between his own personality and nature in a most general, active and harmonious form.'[2]

The aim of education, according to Humboldt, was '*Bildung*': self-cultivation, but for a purpose that went beyond the self and was for the benefit of humanity. Humboldt also envisaged a research-driven purpose for universities and that there would be links between teaching and research. Humboldt's idea was not, strictly speaking, an argument for liberal education, as the pursuit of knowledge he endorsed could be narrow and specialised. Humboldt came to influence the development of research-led rather than liberal higher education. The British philosopher of education David Carr argues that 'insofar as liberal education concerns broad and "holistic" study, avoiding narrow specialisation, it is not reducible to any research-driven pursuit of knowledge' (Carr, 2009: 9).

The Industrial Revolution

It was over four hundred years before other universities emerged in England, with London University (later University College, London) founded in 1826 and the University of Durham founded in 1832. The founding purpose of the University of Durham remained the pursuit of broad-based, often religious, knowledge for the tiny proportion of the male population who resided within the institution and dedicated themselves to a life of scholarship. London University, however, was notably more progressive as it lacked the strong religious focus, offered a wider range of subjects, and study was not dependent upon residence in the institution. It was not until 1871 that UK Parliament passed the Universities Tests Act that decreed that students reading for lay academic degrees did not need to demonstrate active commitment to a particular faith group.

The British Cardinal, John Henry Newman wrote *The Idea of a University* in 1852, in which he described education as its own purpose: 'The principle of real dignity in knowledge, its worth, its desirableness, considered irrespectively of results, is this germ within it of scientific or philosophical process. This is how it comes to be an end in itself; this is why it admits of being called liberal' (Newman, 1959: 138). Newman's belief was that education ran counter to economic utility and that its result should be 'A habit of mind [...] which lasts through life, of which the attributes are freedom, equitableness, calmness, moderation and wisdom [...] a philosophical habit [...] This is the main purpose of a university in its treatment of its students.'[3]

Newman's liberal idea was a major influence upon universities in the UK and was seen by many as standing in opposition to teaching knowledge which could be vocationally useful. However, as Carr indicates, unlike Mill some years later, Newman 'did not deny the significant role of universities in professional training' (Carr, 2009: 3). Rather, his argument was that one would be a better clergyman, lawyer or doctor as a result of a broad-based liberal education. Newman has been criticised for making a 'fraudulent promise' which universities adopted; namely, that if left to pursue knowledge as an end in itself, universities would also provide society with what is useful, and that for individuals, cultivating disinterestedness was the way to achieve self-interested ends (Maskell and Robinson, 2002: 31). However, in contrast to today's impoverished rhetoric of 'employability skills', Newman's vision is liberal indeed.

After Newman, it was left to British poet and school inspector Matthew Arnold (1822–88) to take up the baton for liberal education. Arnold's book *Culture and Anarchy* (1869) defines liberal education in opposition to vocational training. His main argument was that education offered youngsters initiation into the culture of their society – culture being defined as 'the best that has been thought and said in the world' (Carr, 2009: 3). Arnold considered culture to play an important role in unifying society by 'releasing the best instincts of each class and harmoniously integrating them' (O'Hear, 2001: 124).

It is worth revisiting the philosophical ideas behind this liberal ideal of the non-instrumental, disinterested pursuit of knowledge, as they formed the basis of much modern higher education in the western world and can serve as a reminder of the values upon which universities, particularly in Britain, were built, even if they never quite lived up to them. More serious arguments to reconcile tensions between liberal and vocational approaches to education began to be made from the turn of the twentieth century in the writings of, for example, American educational philosopher John Dewey. Many have since argued that the dichotomy between liberal and vocational education, which has persisted to this day, is false (notably Pring, 1995, 2004; Winch, 2000, 2002).

Newman and Arnold perhaps felt compelled to define liberal education as a reaction to the impact of the Industrial Revolution, which began in the UK from the end of the eighteenth century and in America some years later. In many ways Arnold's *Culture and Anarchy* can be seen as a response to this social change, a reaction to industrial progress and the emergent working class. Some sections of the British upper class feared the emergent working class as uncivilised, a state which they believed could be overcome through education and engagement in a unifying culture. Arnold believed all social classes to be capable of appreciating high culture in terms of music, literature and arts, and that giving all citizens access to 'the best that had been thought' would prevent political unrest or social anarchy. From the mid-nineteenth century onwards, industrial and economic development led to the beginnings of calls to increase university places and an increased challenge to the idea that education should have no practical utility. One consequence was the establishment of many new institutions; the 'red-brick' universities in the UK and the 'land-grant' universities in the USA.

In Britain, many of the higher education institutions founded at this time were financed entirely through the donations of wealthy industrialists. Josiah Mason founded a College of Science in Birmingham in the UK in 1880, which later became the prestigious red-brick Birmingham University. Mason was 'deeply convinced of the necessity and benefit of systematic scientific instruction especially adapted to the practical, mechanical and industrial pursuits of the Midlands district' (in Roderick and Stephens, 1981: 240). Businessmen and industrialists from large northern industrial cities, the hotbed of the industrial revolution, perceived the need to provide scientific education for their citizens. In Leeds, businessmen established the Yorkshire College of Science in 1874 which later became Leeds University; in Manchester, Owens College was established but not initially well-funded, as it tried to imitate the liberal curricula of Oxford and Cambridge: 'it was not until relevance to industry was established that gifts began to flow in,'[4] and it went on to become Manchester University.

There is some debate as to whether new universities at this time were established in order to support industrial and therefore economic development through scientific and technological advance, or whether the increased national prosperity through industrial development meant that there was, as a result, more money available to invest in the 'luxury' of universities. This is not just an issue of university funding but a more fundamental question about the purpose of higher education at this time. Some wealthy industrialists sought a university education for their sons so they could better understand the science behind the industry and develop profitable technological advances; for others, university was an indulgent opportunity for their sons to enjoy a status-conferring break before entering the 'real world' as confirmed members of the upper, or at very least professional, class.

It was only when these colleges of science broadened the curriculum out to offer a liberal education to complement the scientific and vocational that the title of a university was conferred by government, perhaps lending support to arguments that 'a nation gets rich then uses some of the wealth to endow more universities, not as engines of economic growth but as centres of piety, learning and thought' (Maskell and Robinson, 2002: 4). This took place in the final two decades of the nineteenth century, which also suggests that although there was an emergent trend to link education (especially science) to industry and to the economy, universities were still considered largely outside this pursuit of interest. The by now 'ancient' universities of Oxford and Cambridge, Durham and London largely stayed away from teaching science and technology and continued to offer the liberal curriculum espoused by Newman and Arnold. Technically, Oxbridge accounted for 80 per cent of science graduates in 1890, although these were all in the field of mathematics.

To counterpose the liberal ancients against the vocational red-bricks ignores the important role that older universities played in 'training' young men to enter the professions – not just the Church, but also law and medicine. Through this training, universities conferred social status upon graduates or acted as an early means of social mobility, despite this never having been their prime motivation. Portraying opposition between liberal and vocational aims in higher education at this time also ignores the fact that the 'vocational' offer causing so much discussion was largely an avowedly academic and disinterested study of science. Although designed from the outset 'to give such technical instruction as would be of immediate service in professional and commercial life' (Roderick and Stephens, 1974: 41), courses in physics, chemistry and geology would today be considered 'pure' science and solely academic. Similarly, even courses in engineering, mining and metallurgy, although of perhaps more direct practical utility, would still be academically rigorous.

Public and private funding

In America at this time, similar tensions between the liberal and vocational were in play. There was already a distinction emerging between privately funded universities such as Harvard and Yale, and state-funded universities such as the University of Georgia, founded in 1785. The state-funded universities increased in number with the passing of the Morrill Act (also known as the 'Land Grant Act') by federal government in 1862. This act granted states 30,000 acres of land for each state representative in Congress to sell to fund educational institutions whose prime purpose would be the teaching of subjects related to 'agriculture and mechanical arts'. The aim of the act was to promote the education of the 'industrial classes'.

The thirteenth amendment finally ended slavery in every state in 1865, three years after the Morrill Act. However, it was not until the passing of a second Morrill Act, in 1890, that public money began to be used to fund university places specifically for black students. The second Morrill Act led to the creation of sixteen new land-grant colleges, which have become historically associated with black students. 'Land-grant' universities, such as the University of Florida or Colorado State University, initially served the sons and daughters of wealthier farm workers and an emerging working class. Private universities, free from state interference, were able to continue offering a more liberal curriculum. As in Britain, it was not long before the new higher education institutions developed liberal arts components so that they could offer programmes similar to those at private universities.

In both Britain and America, it seems that a generation of parents who made money from agriculture or industry in the middle of the nineteenth century were keen for their own children to receive the education, and associated social status, that they never had. Although some governments, states and wealthy benefactors may have wished to see the development of scientific and practical education to drive forward industrial advancement, institutions in both countries sought to complement scientific courses with a more liberal offer through arts and humanities subjects, and this was necessary in order for them to receive the title 'university'.

From this historical discussion of the establishment of 'red-brick' universities in Britain and 'land-grant' universities in America, we can see that what on the surface appears to be a discussion about the structure, funding and content of higher education 'has already become deeply enmeshed with concerns about economic and industrial, demographic and moral transformations' (Silver, 1983: 154). Although there was pressure to develop scientific and technical education, there was also pressure to safeguard and build upon existing university values. As the British historian Harold Silver points out, it could be seen that the 'new' universities which began to appear in both America and Britain towards the end of the nineteenth century actually served to protect the existing universities, by removing from them the pressure to adapt to a changing social, economic and political climate. This allowed science and technology to be taught in other institutions whilst preserving the liberal ideal in a parallel system of historically more established universities.[5]

In America, the Morrill Act provided generous financial support for universities, and this demonstrated the commitment of federal government to the higher education sector overall. In particular, public money was used to encourage the establishment of institutions offering a more vocationally oriented curriculum. The first grants from the British government to universities were made in 1889, but this was only after the civic colleges had been well established through private and local corporation money and begun to 'liberalise'. In 1889 a grant of £15,000 was given to such institutions (Roderick and Stephens, 1981: 240) and this represented one-third of their total funding, the other two-thirds coming, in roughly equal measure, from individual fees and private donations (Carpentier, 2011).

The drive amongst American universities to compete against each other for market share of students first became established after the second

Morrill Act and the emergence of a greater number of universities. The American writer and former President of Harvard University, Derek Bok, notes that at the turn of the twentieth century the University of Chicago began advertising to attract students, and the University of Pennsylvania launched a 'Bureau of Publicity' to raise its profile. As President Andrew Draper of the University of Illinois observed in 1906, the university 'is a business concern as well as a moral and intellectual instrumentality, and if business methods are not applied to its management it will break down.'[6]

It was also at this time that American universities first began to consider the profile of campus sports as integral to their reputation. In 1905, Harvard was concerned enough about its profitable football team to hire a 26-year-old coach at a salary equal to that of its president and twice the amount paid to its full professors (Bok, 2005: 2). Sporting success was considered particularly important for universities who saw their target market as national, or indeed international, rather than just the local community. Sporting success would raise the profile of an institution and attract more fee-paying students. However, this came at a cost, as in return universities had to spend increasingly large sums of money on sports facilities and coaching staff. Such an emphasis on sport co-existed alongside an academic curriculum. It is worth stressing that, at this point, the nascent marketisation of American universities did not signify an end to liberal education or the emergence of the student as consumer.

We have already seen how, with the passage of the Morrill Act, government funding of universities took place slightly earlier in America than it did in Britain. The federal government wanted vocational education enough to pay for it, and the Morrill Act 'was not intended to promote pure knowledge, but rather to serve the states' (Tuchman, 2009: 205). Pressure for liberal alternatives to agriculture and mechanics came from students and their families, the states, and the already-established institutions. Federal government had to pass the Smith-Hughes Act in 1917 to provide money for specifically vocational training schemes in US universities (Silver, 1983: 165). From this point, near the end of the First World War, the British government began to look to debates and evidence emerging from the USA to lend support to its arguments for an increasingly vocational curriculum in schools and colleges, although, initially at least, it held back from applying these arguments to the more protected environment of the universities.

National economic competitiveness

At the heart of both the British and the American governments' concern to encourage universities to serve an increasingly vocational purpose was the issue of national economic competitiveness. Whereas Britain had passed through an industrial revolution ahead of other countries it became increasingly difficult to maintain economic growth rates, and industrialisation in other countries soon led to the development of more efficient means of production elsewhere in the world. Higher education and the growth of a skilled workforce was seen by the UK government as one answer to the country's lack of economic competitiveness. In 1920, the British government established the University Grants Committee to secure the funding of HE, and by 1921 university funding had shifted to almost 50 per cent from government, 36 per cent from individual fees and the remainder from private donations (Carpentier, 2011).

On both sides of the Atlantic, demands from national government to increase the reach of HE were only partially successful, as they ran counter to individual expectations that a university place would confer social status upon the son of a man who had made his money through industry. For universities to play this social role they needed to maintain exclusivity. British historian Eric Hobsbawm indicates that 'the number of students in universities, which offered a guarantee of middle-class membership, approximately tripled in most European countries between the late 1870s and 1913' (Hobsbawm, 1987: 177). Instead of such growth being universally welcomed, universities sought to protect their exclusivity through limiting entry.

In the USA, Scholastic Aptitude Tests (SATs) were first introduced in 1926, which set a benchmark level of ability for entry to particular universities. Entry then became dependent upon demonstration of prior educational attainment which, some argue, could be successfully coached in secondary schools. Hobsbawm tells us that a body of private secondary schools, mainly in the northeast of the USA 'prepared the sons of good, or at any rate rich, families for the final polish of private elite universities.'[7] This is similar to the long-established and misleadingly named small network of elite 'public' schools in the UK, from which Oxford and Cambridge chiefly recruited. At this time Cambridge University also introduced school leaving qualifications to provide the university with an indication of a candidate's prior educational attainment. However such tests could be bypassed through performing well at interview or having a recommendation from an influential family friend.

In the UK, entry to the middle class through education was certainly possible at this time and the scholarships provided primarily by philanthropists enabled exceptionally bright working-class youngsters to take up places. However, scholarship students comprised a tiny proportion of the university population, partly due to the lack of publicly funded secondary schooling. In general, universities were used more to maintain the position of the established social elite rather than to 'promote' the sons and daughters of workers. The reputation of Oxford and Cambridge perhaps emerged as a way of controlling entry to the middle class even amongst graduates. People who had obtained a university degree elsewhere 'found it advisable to take a further degree or examination at Oxbridge'.[8]

When the numbers entering university continued to increase, other informal mechanisms of denoting social standing were organised through education. In Britain, certain Oxbridge colleges were considered more prestigious than others; in America, the more elite universities were denoted by the sports they played against each other in the 'Ivy League'. However, in general, the HE system in America was significantly more socially open than the system in the UK. As an example, we can see that in 1910 there were 56,000 women at universities in the USA compared with a little over 1,000 in the UK. The first university (liberal arts college) for women was founded in the USA in 1766, whereas the first women's college at Cambridge, Girton College, was not founded until 100 years after this.

There were increased political and economic demands to expand education in the years after the First World War. Despite military victory, Britain's position at the head of a global empire no longer seemed so secure, and political intentions to expand access to education were thwarted by the economic downturn of the 1920s. The Fisher Education Act of 1918 made education compulsory until the age of fourteen, although this was not implemented until 1921; even then there was little money to expand secondary education, and few people gained the entry qualifications necessary for university. Despite an increase in the provision of scholarships to academically talented youngsters from less wealthy backgrounds, universities remained largely the preserve of the upper classes. In the absence of public money, there was little pressure upon universities to change their curricula and the classical liberal education that had been studied for generations continued to be offered, despite an awareness of the technology and science studied at high levels in the competitor countries such as the USA and Germany. The preparations for war in the 1930s took political attention away from education, and the Second World War then took a generation of potential scholars and lecturers away from universities.

The post-war expansion of higher education

After the Second World War there was intense pressure to reform education at all levels. More people wanted access to HE and it became increasingly difficult for governments to justify institutions that served such a small minority of the population. Returning servicemen in the USA and the UK wanted to take up university places interrupted by the war, and men who would not have been able to afford university before the war wanted access to the opportunities available to their battlefield peers. Likewise British women, having won the right to suffrage in 1928 and having played a major role on the home front during the Second World War, were not prepared to retreat to the domestic sphere but sought more equal access to the same educational opportunities as men. The old social hierarchies were called into question.

In the USA, pressure to expand access to universities was first met with the Serviceman's Readjustment Act of 1944, known as the GI Bill. The GI Bill allowed returning servicemen preferential access to employment, education and training alongside financial support to enable them to take advantage of such opportunities. These benefits were offered initially for a seven-year period, and almost eight million veterans took advantage of the scheme, of which more than two million took up a place at college or university. This led to a near-doubling of the college population and started to challenge the link between a university place and family wealth. There were few direct grants given to institutions, and much of the increased government funding for universities was channelled through students themselves. This reinforced the establishment of the university market and further encouraged institutions to compete for individual students. After the Second World War, this competition between institutions became more meaningful with cheaper and faster transport links between states and nationally implemented SATs, which broke the link between particular schools and universities.

By 1946, with thousands of veterans entering universities and colleges, President Truman launched a Commission on Higher Education to examine the role of colleges and universities. The *Truman Commission Report* was published in 1947 and recommended significant changes, including doubling college enrolments by 1960 and extending free public higher education through the establishment of a network of community colleges. Community colleges provide two-year Associate degree programmes in any subject deemed to be in demand by the local community, and allow students to transfer to state universities and 'trade up' their Associate degree to a full Bachelor's degree. However, community colleges have always suffered from lower status than the private and state universities. The American sociologist David Riesman is critical of the fact that 'basket weaving earns as many credits as physical chemistry' (Reisman, 1998: 179). In effect, Truman established a two-tier binary system of HE.

The political will to expand HE in America at this point was being driven by the Cold War and, in particular, the space race. In 1957 the National Defense Education Act was passed and this authorised increased funding for scientific research and science education. When the Soviet Union in 1961 became the first country in the world to send a man into space, this led to fear that the USA was falling behind its international rivals, and expanding HE was seen as one means of winning the competition. More money in HE meant that the number of universities, the number of places for students, and the number of scholarships available could expand. This not only led to a large overall increase in student numbers but also to a change in the social composition of the university. HE was no longer the preserve of the wealthy.

Truman's 1947 expectations were surpassed and the 1960s witnessed a five-fold increase in the number of students attending community colleges, attracting working-class students who had not previously had opportunity to experience HE. In part the growth in student numbers experienced in the USA was due to a growing trend towards 'credentialism': more jobs required applicants to hold university degrees. Post-school qualifications increasingly became a prerequisite for employment of any sort. At the same time, political changes such as the success of the civil rights movement meant more black students were able to take up university places.

The Higher Education Act of 1965 formed part of President Lyndon Johnson's 'war on poverty', aiming to widen the opportunities for low-income students through an increase in federal aid to universities. There was an assumption that providing citizens with HE would enable them to secure remunerative employment. However, the decision to distribute a large proportion of this money through scholarships and student loans rather than through direct payment to institutions further enhanced the 'market' in recruiting students. There were significant sums of money in higher education; students just had to be persuaded to spend their share with particular universities. Tuition fees at public universities were not considered a barrier to entry at this time as many state universities 'kept tuition artificially low by not indexing it to inflation'.[9] Students soon came to realise they were in a powerful position.

Inequalities persisted however, as a Basic Education Opportunity Grant paid students 'less than half of stated tuition, not leaving anything for living expenses in a residential institution'.[10] Many scholarships, although financially supported by federal government, were administered and distributed by states that, fearing a 'brain drain', sought to keep students in-state and therefore awarded the largest scholarships or fee-reductions to students attending their 'local' institution. Many state universities were required by law to offer a place to all high school graduates, and later community colleges offered places to mature students who had not completed high school (known as 'open admission'). The total number of graduates, from private and public institutions, was controlled not so much by entry requirements as by progression rates once students had embarked upon a programme of study. Attrition rates of 50 per cent were considered normal.[11] The increase in student numbers was reflected in a rise in the number of institutions, and today there are more than 9,700 colleges and universities in the USA.

Private universities needed to reconsider their offer in the light of this public expansion. The exclusivity of higher academic entry requirements and larger tuition fees as well as the cost of residential accommodation ensured the prestige of degrees from private universities. The major Ivy League universities, which attracted students from across the country, could demand the highest tuition fees and the highest SATs scores and maintain exclusivity in a way that other universities – and especially community colleges – could not. There were conflicting tensions between allowing universities to operate according to a 'free market' and increasing state regulation. The channelling of financial support through students paved the way for universities to step up the marketing strategies they had already begun to pursue, while the increase in the number of institutions led to further awareness of the commercial potential of the sector.

In the USA by this point, higher education was no longer experienced as one market with institutions competing for the same pool of students, but as 'many markets where very different colleges and universities market different products to different consumers' (Morphew and Taylor, 2011: 53). Universities spent ever-larger sums of money on publicity and recruitment, which ultimately needed to be paid for by the students themselves through increased tuition fees or decreased services (Riesman, 1998: 121). The period from 1965 to 1980 is noted by Riesman as the period in the history of American HE in which the student consumer was created.

In the UK during this period many similar influences held sway. Despite pressure to increase the scope and range of the HE sector, many potential new students were disappointed to encounter the same universities they had left before the outbreak of World War Two. A 'tripartite' secondary school system was implemented after the war as part of the Butler Act of 1944. This placed children at age eleven into a grammar, technical or secondary modern school, based upon the results of a selection test. This made the high-level academic education required for university entrance accessible to a small number of students from working-class backgrounds. However, students were financially dependent upon either the private means of their families or, if exceptionally talented, the generosity of entrepreneurs and philanthropists who provided scholarships. As a result many universities remained socially elite.

In 1945–6 there were just 40,000 UK university students, and despite post-war expansion, even by 1962 just four per cent of school leavers attended university.[12] In both Britain and America the rapidly increasing population as a result of the post-war 'baby boom' meant that even maintaining the same proportion of the population at university as before the war necessitated extra provision. The high cost of war to the British economy in particular meant that expansion of HE in the UK was slower than across the Atlantic. Although politicians in the UK were influenced by the implementation of the *Truman Commission Report*, government money was prioritised elsewhere, in setting up the Welfare State and the National Health Service. The *Anderson Report* of 1960 recommended that government should increase the finance available to higher education, including the establishment of new institutions. This instigated initially slow growth within the HE sector. In 1962 permission was given for the establishment of 'new' universities to be built on greenfield sites around the UK at places such as Warwick, Lancaster and Canterbury.

It was not until the Education Act of 1962 that money was available to require Local Education Authorities (LEAs) in the UK to provide universities with the full cost of students' tuition fees and students themselves with means-tested grants for living expenses. In 1963, the economist Baron Lionel Robbins wrote a government-commissioned report on the future of HE, in which he argued for the expansion of the sector and, significantly, that people from more diverse social backgrounds with 'ability and attainment' should be given the opportunity to study at university level. Robbins argued that there was a need for 'increased attention to including young men and women from families with scant educational background',[13] pointing out that working-class 'grammar-school boys' may not perform as well at university admission interviews as their middle-class, perhaps privately educated peers. The *Robbins Report* came out of a period of relative economic prosperity and social pressure to liberalise opportunities to more people in society; despite this, however, Robbins suggested that students should contribute up to 20 per cent of the cost of their university tuition fees.

The economic prosperity of the early 1960s was built upon developments in industry and manufacturing. In 1963 British Prime Minister-elect Harold Wilson made a speech hailing the age of the 'white heat of technology'. Robbins argued for educational expansion as a means of capitalising upon scientific and technological advance that would in turn have a direct impact upon the national economy and help the UK maintain competitiveness. However, Robbins also considered a more highly educated population to be a good thing in and of itself. Robbins maintained a belief in the concept of liberal education, writing: '[The] search for truth is an essential function of the institutions of higher education, and the process of education is itself most vital when it partakes in the nature of discovery'.[14] Robbins' plan was for a strong disciplinary focus to building knowledge within universities.

Robbins shared a belief, originating from Matthew Arnold, that disseminating high culture could bind the nation and bring together people from different social classes. Because education could play a role in building the national economy and bringing together the nation, it came to be conceived of as a 'public good' whose benefits reached far beyond individual students attending university. Government money was committed to funding universities and providing many students with generous maintenance grants. Such grants were means-tested on the basis of parental income, and students from wealthy families received little or no state funding for living costs, although all tuition costs were met by the LEA. The introduction of such grants did an enormous amount to increase the number of students attending university overall and to make university places available to students who would not have otherwise have been able to take advantage of them.

Class, race and sex

In both the UK and the USA, there was an increase in the number of young people seeking to apply to university as the post-war baby-boom generation came of age. In 1955 there were about 620,000 eighteen-year-olds in the UK; by 1965, that figure had reached 963,000 (Ross, 2003: 14). This meant that although the total number of university places increased overall, it was a long time before there was a noticeable increase in the proportion of the population attending university. The UK was a society still divided by social class hierarchies, and the educational ambitions of many youngsters in the 1960s were to remain thwarted. For young people from families that depended upon them earning a wage at the earliest available opportunity, staying on at school beyond the school leaving age of fifteen was difficult, and it was not until 1973 that the school leaving age was raised to sixteen. Although there were moves towards developing comprehensive secondary schools which could be attended by any pupil irrespective of ability, the division at age eleven between those attending academic grammar schools and vocational secondary modern schools persisted in many areas. Almost from inception, there was criticism that too often the tripartite school system merely divided children along social class lines. It was argued that a disproportionately high number of middle-class children won coveted places at grammar schools, with their promise of educational and social advancement usually starting with a university place. This will be returned to when we consider the decisions taken by the Labour government with Anthony Crosland as Secretary of State for Education in 1965.

American society at this time was divided by race as well as by social class. The burgeoning civil rights movement of the 1960s challenged the inferior status of black citizens, particularly in the South, where many American schools were divided along colour lines. Segregation meant that black and white children were educated in different schools, with the schools for black children often having a higher teacher-pupil ratio, fewer books, poor buildings, and a lack of equipment. Long after segregation was legally challenged it continued informally, with white parents moving out of previously racially mixed areas in order to secure places for their children in predominantly white schools. In 1971 the Supreme Court controversially ruled that forced 'bussing' be employed to achieve a degree of racial desegregation.

Segregation continued into HE, with a demarcation between historically black and white universities. Cheyney University in Pennsylvania, established in 1837, was the first black university, but most historically black HE institutions emerged first after the American Civil War of 1861–5. Blacks had to exert a great deal of political pressure to secure parity of funding with historically white universities, which did not happen to any great extent until after the passing of the second Morrill Act. Such racial distinctions persisted because of the geographical areas in which universities were built, the composition of the faculty and the pervasive influence of religion: white churches supported universities for white students. As in the UK, finance, fear of prejudice and personal aspiration clearly played a role in influencing student choice of institution. For many black students, the prospect of entering an Ivy League residential university far from home was considered financially unaffordable and socially unrealistic. The civil rights movement in America began to challenge this segregation and to open up the possibility of a more equal HE system.

Students used their power within universities and colleges to challenge the political, social and cultural inequalities of the time. There were, for example, calls by students to abolish SATs entry tests on the grounds that these were unfair and culturally biased. There was increased pressure for universities to exercise positive discrimination or affirmative action to provide more opportunities for black students, particularly those from more economically disadvantaged backgrounds. By 1967 such institutional policies began to have an impact, and an increasing number of black students were recruited to universities. American academic and social commentator Allan Bloom laments the fact that in order to achieve greater representation of black students, 'standards of admission had silently and drastically been altered' (Bloom, 1987: 94).

Faced with a choice between failing large numbers of students, lowering academic standards, or providing more intensive academic support, universities looked to the emerging Black Power movement for a politically acceptable solution and offered what would, in effect, become culturally segregated courses in 'black studies and black English' (Bloom, 1987: 94). Bloom notes that black students at Cornell University became aware that they 'were not just students but negotiating partners in the process of determining what an education is', and that this led to 'permanent quotas in admission, preference in financial assistance, racially motivated hiring of faculty, difficulty in giving blacks failing marks, and an organised system of grievance and feeling aggrieved' (Bloom, 1987: 95).

Feminism was another movement for change that had an impact on university campuses in both the USA and the UK. In the UK in 1961, female students were a distinct minority in universities; the student body was 71 per cent male and 29 per cent female. Throughout the 1960s and 1970s the assumption that boys and girls should be educated separately, in single-sex schools offering distinct curricula, was challenged, and by 1979 the male/female university student ratio was 60:40 (Ross, 2003: 54). Similarly in America, although the proportion of women entering universities had always been higher than in the UK, many had been taught in single-sex institutions, but the feminist movement challenged this assumption and saw single-sex colleges decline in popularity, mainly through male colleges admitting female students rather than the other way round.

The Vietnam War brought further change to universities in America. There was an increase in college enrolment from 1969, as HE provided a legitimate means of avoiding conscription into the army. There are suggestions of 'grade inflation' occurring at this time, as lecturers realised that failing students might have led to them being forced to withdraw from university and face military service. Widespread student protests had occurred on university campuses in the years preceding the Vietnam War. One major protest was the Berkeley Free Speech Movement, which started in the autumn of 1964 in response to students being prevented from distributing publicity and collecting money for civil rights causes by university officials.

The University of Berkeley's President, Clark Kerr, was criticised by student leaders for running the university as a business. Hundreds of protest marches, rallies and occupations took place over many months and led to a rescinding of the ban on political activity and the eventual firing of President Kerr. The mass student protests over the war in Vietnam galvanised existing discontent and reinforced the sense that through exercising their collective power, students could successfully make demands of the college hierarchies and have their voices heard. This was a lesson that stuck long after the war in Vietnam had ended.

Students became in effect negotiating partners in determining the form and content of education, and many academics were unable or unwilling to defend the disciplinary knowledge content of their curricula. This is problematic because, as will be discussed more fully in Chapter Four, students by definition having not yet completed their education are not in a strong position to determine what this education should be. The inability of the academy to challenge this assumption contributes to the construction of students as consumers.

Yet rather than challenging the concept of students as negotiating partners in constructing educational curricula, liberal attention has focused upon the abhorrence of the commercialisation of the campus. Commercial practices, although employed by many institutions prior to 1970, reached unprecedented size and scope in subsequent years. Bok notes that before 1970, universities were not averse to advertising and using other business methods, but commercialisation, which he defines as selling the work of the university to make a profit, was confined to the periphery of the campus: athletics programmes and perhaps extension programmes or correspondence courses. From 1970 onwards such practices really took off.

Human capital theory and HE markets

The writing of both the *Robbins Report* and the *Truman Commission Report* occurred against a backdrop of relative economic prosperity and an appetite for social change. In the UK this was already beginning to diminish by the time the *Robbins Report* was published. The Conservative government that commissioned the report was voted out of office in the general election of 1964, and it was left to the Labour Party to implement Robbins' proposals. Anthony Crosland became Secretary of State for Education in 1965, and he did not support the expansion of the universities, regarding them as 'over-protected and over-resourced in comparison with other [education] demands' (Gordon et al., 1991: 242). Furthermore, the idea that universities were autonomous institutions outside of the control of LEAs, unlike teacher training colleges or further education colleges, added another reason for the Labour Party's political distaste.

Crosland considered, perhaps rightly, that the education system in the UK, from the tripartite division of pupils aged eleven to the wealth and autonomy of the universities, was elitist and socially divisive, serving only to confirm the status of the middle and upper classes. Rather than seeking to drive up educational achievement in schools and enabling more working-class children to access a high quality academic curriculum such as on offer in grammar schools and subsequently universities, Crosland decided to abolish the entire system. He saw his first priority in office as the dismantling of the grammar schools, and then ruled out any expansion of the universities for ten years. Instead, Crosland proposed to create a binary HE sector (ironically what he sought to abolish in schools) with the creation of a different set of institutions: the polytechnics. The idea was that, unlike community colleges in the USA, polytechnics and universities would be equal in status but different in purpose.

The UK government's policy document, *A Plan for Polytechnics and Other Colleges*, was published in 1965 and proposed the creation of thirty polytechnics, which would award degrees accredited by the Council for National Academic Awards. From the outset the idea was that polytechnics would offer different forms of HE to different types of students (Ross, 2003: 49). They were to focus on meeting the technological needs of industry and to offer access to HE to mature and part-time students. Crosland's aim had been to create Higher Education Institutions (HEIs) outside of the university hierarchy, but perhaps comparisons were inevitable. Polytechnics were not as generously funded as the universities and accepted students with lower-level entry qualifications than many of the universities. Consequently, the degrees they offered, particularly in academic subjects, were not always seen as equivalent to those offered by the universities.

Polytechnics did offer a more vocational curriculum, but they soon began to teach academic subjects too. They opened up more places for female and mature students, but also created far more places for 'traditional' students. By 1979 the proportion of school-leavers in HE in the UK had increased to 10 per cent of the population. As we first saw with the emergence of the red-brick universities and the teaching of science, the technical and vocational curriculum becoming the provenance of the polytechnics left universities free to pursue liberal programmes. For many bright working-class youngsters, it was still the case that attending an elite university seemed an insurmountable social and financial challenge.

As the 1960s drew to a close, the economic downturn of the 1970s began to call into question the role of HE once more. One idea that came into ascendancy with the demise of the liberal conception of HE was human capital theory, which emerged from the USA in the early 1970s and gained in popularity round the world as a means of exploring how capitalism could move beyond the limits of economic growth that were being perceived at that time. American economist Theodore Schultz describes 'the role of the acquired abilities of human agents as a major source of the unexplained gains in productivity' (Schultz, 1971: v), and identifies investment in human capital as taking many forms but including 'schooling and higher education, on the job training, migration, health and economic information.'[15] It is probably no coincidence that economically, this was a period of emerging recession, which came to be defined by the 1973 oil crisis. The era of cheap energy and cheap industrialisation was coming to an end, and efforts to intensify the production process in order to increase profitability led to a focus upon people and the potential to increase the rate of production through human, rather than economic, capital.

The concept of human capital was of most interest to 'right-wing' economists because it was based upon the idea that each individual had the freedom to invest in himself: 'It is one way free men can enhance their welfare.'[16] Education thus comes to be 'an investment activity undertaken for the purpose of acquiring capabilities that enhance future earnings of the person as a productive agent'.[17] This was seen to operate on both an individual and a national level; just as individuals could invest in their own personal skills levels, so too could nations invest in the skills of their people.

Despite many critiques of human capital theory, which have focused upon the emotional abhorrence of considering people as crude economic investments, there continued to be political enthusiasm for this perception of education. It was just three years after the oil crisis on 18 October 1976 that then UK Prime Minister James Callaghan spoke at Ruskin College of the need for education to equip children 'to do a job of work'. This was just over a decade after the publication of the *Robbins Report*, which propounded predominantly liberal values of HE; yet the recession of the 1970s made the world seem a very different place to the more prosperous 1960s. The American sociologist Ivar Berg was critical of the effect of such suggestions upon education at this time, and *The Great Training Robbery* highlights some of the dangers of accepting 'a mechanistic interpretation of the relationship between education and employment' (Berg, 1971: 6). Despite this, the concept of human capital has retained popularity with some government ministers and economists in the intervening decades

Early exponents of human capital theory still held onto a belief that HE was a public good; it would be the national economy that would benefit from more productive workers. Since 1979 there has been a slow shift away from the perception of HE as a public good with its purpose either a liberal search for truth in knowledge or for knowledge to drive forward scientific and technological advance for the national economy. From 1979 it became increasingly obvious that the economy was heading for another downturn, and in Britain this year saw the election of a Conservative government and Margaret Thatcher as Prime Minister. In the early 1980s real-term financial cutbacks were planned for the HE sector in the UK, fewer places made available for students, and lecturers were made redundant. All over the UK the heavy industries of ship-building, coal-mining and steel-making were closing down forever, and when the economy began to recover in the mid–1980s it was decidedly 'post-industrial', based largely on a service sector of banking, retail, call centres and emerging new technologies.

Post-industrialism and the 'knowledge economy'

It was in this context that the concept of the 'knowledge economy' began to come to the fore. This was very different from the first half of the twentieth century, where the view had been that knowledge was necessary for scientific and technological advancement, and it was scientific discoveries and new technologies that would drive forward the economy. Now the idea was that knowledge itself would become a valuable commodity, the knowledge embodied within individuals in the form of human capital. This marked the start of the transition from HE being seen as a public good to being conceived of as a private good. It was no longer considered to be society that benefited from the skills of graduates; rather, the benefit was seen as a purely individual one, in the form of increased earning potential. This led to an increasingly instrumental perception of the purpose of higher education as being directly linked to future employment prospects. American economist Gary Becker introduces his third edition of *Human Capital* with the argument that 'Education and training are the most important investments in human capital [...] high school and college education in the US greatly raises a person's income' (Becker, 1993). If it was graduates who benefited from attending university with the reward of higher wages, it became increasingly difficult to argue the case for fully funding an HE sector at the taxpayers' expense.

In America, the free market for students both between and within institutions did not necessarily deliver what the federal government had hoped for. The state of the national HE sector was clearly a government concern and in 1980, under President Carter, the Department for Education became a Cabinet-level agency for the first time. This decision reflects the political concerns at this time regarding economic slowdown and industrial competition, particularly from Japan and parts of Europe. It was considered increasingly important to link higher education to business. The Bayh-Dole Act of 1980 enabled universities to profit from securing patents on scientific discoveries that public money had made possible. The decision was also taken at this time to provide federal aid to fund teaching and therefore to reduce the costs of university admission, making HE more affordable to more of the population. However, such financial support arguably had little impact upon facilitating access: 'low costs did not facilitate access in the pre-Regan era nor have increasingly high costs deterred demand in the post-Regan period' (Brown, 2011: 174). Nor did these changes slow down the commercialisation of the HE sector; in fact, the impact of the Bayh-Dole Act was to hasten the drive to make a profit. Bok argues that this was due to the rapid growth of opportunities 'to supply education, expert advice, and scientific knowledge in return for handsome sums of money' (Bok, 2005: 10).

The impact of the market was no longer confined to competition between institutions but became an important influence within institutions too. Academic departments and lecturers had to compete against each other to retain their market share of the student body. At many universities, students were offered places on the college board so that institutions could better understand what students wanted from their experience and respond accordingly. University administrators became charged with responding to student demand through an 'ability to change the inventory rapidly, as some "product lines" appear to sell more quickly while others move slowly or not at all' (Riesman, 1998: 196). It is this move fundamentally to alter the content, structure and assessment of education to meet student demands that consolidates students as consumers far more than funding arrangements. However, this response to student choice is linked to the need for institutions to make money, and such market responsiveness is pursued rigorously by academic and administrative staff as an essential function of their role (Bok, 2005).

The British government proposed university tuition fees at this point, but the suggestion was so politically unpopular with the electorate (and especially perhaps with the more middle-class core of Conservative party voters) that it was ruled out. Growth of HE began again in the mid–1980s but this time the growth in student numbers outstripped the funding available to HE institutions. The money available for resources, including teaching staff, grew overall but fell in relation to student numbers. This reflected a global trend to argue for (if not necessarily to achieve) reduced public sector expenditure as a whole. In the early 1990s, the World Bank suggested that a US-style, market-driven model of HE be replicated internationally.

Although less well-funded relative to student numbers than its American counterpart, the HE sector in the UK expanded rapidly in the early 1990s. The issue of funding universities again came to the fore; politicians and commentators once more began to ask whether students could reasonably be expected to make a financial contribution to the cost of an education from which they were considered to be the chief beneficiaries. Moves in this direction first occurred with the Education Act of 1990, which legislated for the freezing (and eventual phasing out) of means-tested maintenance grants for living expenses; the establishment of the Student Loans Company (SLC); and the replacement of student grants with student loans. This legislation encapsulated a final challenge to the notion that HE was a public good worth subsidising from the public purse.

Two years later, the Further and Higher Education Act retracted Labour's 1965 legislation and brought to an end the binary divide between universities and polytechnics. Now, after successfully completing an application process, all HE institutions could call themselves universities and award their own undergraduate degrees. The 1992 Act also introduced more competition for funding between institutions, particularly in the area of research. Funding for teaching became more closely linked to student numbers, although universities were told by central government how many students they were permitted to recruit. This served to open up a limited form of university marketplace and, for the first time, made advertising and promotion a serious concern of institutions. A generation of eighteen-year-old university applicants (and, perhaps more importantly, their parents) had grown up with the concept of educational choice, having been encouraged to exercise their 'right to choose' primary and secondary schools, and were not perturbed by an HE market.

In 1993 the Conservative government, surprised by re-election in 1992, published a series of 'charters' to set out what members of the public could expect to receive from state services. On the one hand this can be seen as a crude attempt to win popularity cheaply: nothing more was being promised, people were just being told, in colourful publicity, what they could expect to receive from public services. However, another way of looking at this push for charters was as an attempt to renegotiate the relationship between state and society. In the language of charters, citizens became service-users, clients and customers. This was stated explicitly in the publication of the Student Charter in 1993 – a thin, colourful document aimed at students which provided a formal statement that students were, alongside local businesses, the 'customers' of a university that was intended to 'deliver a service' to them. The impact of this will be discussed more fully in Chapter Four. In 1995 the Departments of Education and Employment were merged to form one new cabinet office, the DfEE, an 'implied cause and effect that Labour were happy to keep' (Maskell and Robinson, 2002: 5).

Conclusion

This brief history shows that higher education in Britain and America has long been subjected to social, political and economic pressures. There have been demands for universities to meet a need for national technological advancement, for example, or to provide a form of social legitimacy for a newly wealthy middle class. Arguments as to whether higher education should be liberal, academic and for the public good, or for individual economic benefit and social mobility, have raged in different forms for well over one hundred years. Running parallel with these debates has been an almost continuous expansion in the number of institutions, lecturers and students. With this expansion has come a growing diversity amongst the student body.

By the mid–1990s, where this chapter ends, arguments had firmly swung in favour of instrumental objectives for higher education. Universities are considered by policy makers to be more about conferring private benefit upon individuals than public benefit upon society as a whole. Alongside this, there are few who defend a concept of education for its own sake nowadays. The idea introduced at the beginning of this chapter, that education is a conversation between the generations, a passing-on of society's collective knowledge for new citizens to make their own, no longer exists in reality. This shift in purpose is perhaps less about changes in universities than about changes in society as a whole. A post-modern assault on the nature of truth and knowledge has combined with the wider crisis of post-industrial society to call into question the very assumption that there is indeed a coherent body of knowledge that is worth preserving and passing on to future generations.

Members of the academy, and the political elite, are no longer confident about asserting a national project in relation to higher education. Knowledge, most specifically in the form of culture, is no longer perceived of as a public good, either in terms of its economic role in building national prosperity or its social role in including all of society into a coherent cultural vision. Universities are no longer routinely concerned with the passing-on of knowledge, through education, to new generations of citizens. This has been replaced by new goals. Now universities are more often charged with serving non-educational purposes relating to individual employ-ability, social inclusion or even personal transformation. How this plays out in practice, and the impact this has upon students, is the focus for the remainder of this book.

Endnotes

1 ACCM Occasional Paper (22).

2 In Hohendorf (2000).

3 Newman (1959), 129.

4 In Roderick and Stephens (1981), 240.

5 Silver (1983), 156.

6 Bok (2005), 2.

7 Hobsbawm (1987), 178.

8 Hobsbawm (1987), 178.

9 Reisman (1998), 160.

10 Reisman (1998), 119.

11 Reisman (1998), 173.

12 Committee on Higher Education (1963).

13 Committee on Higher Education (1963).

14 Committee on Higher Education (1963).

15 Schultz (1971), 8.

16 Schultz (1971), 26.

17 Schultz (1971), 8.

2

The rise of the student consumer

In the period since the mid–1990s, many of the political trends discussed in the previous chapter that led to the creation of a higher education market have escalated. Most recently, alternative political ideas about the purpose of the HE sector, such as a focus upon social inclusion or individual social mobility, have become increasingly influential in both Britain and America. Today politicians are happy to talk of HE as not just enabling social mobility but also of bringing about social justice and a more inclusive society. Yet this apparent balancing of aims towards the social as well as the economic does nothing to slow down the pace at which students are constructed as consumers. In fact, the focus on 'social mobility', in particular, enhances the perception that students are consumers and universities merely service providers.

The period since 1995 is perhaps most notable in the UK for an escalation in the publication and enactment of government policy. More government documents on the topic of HE have been published in the past fifteen years than were published in total up to the Second World War. In 2011 the British government produced the 'White Paper' *Higher Education: Students at the Heart of the System*, setting out the eleventh new 'framework' for the UK HE sector since the Robbins Report of 1963. This means in practice that roughly every three years universities in the UK have undergone fundamental ideological and practical upheavals. Perhaps only the most obvious result of this policy escalation has been an increase in student numbers – up from 1.3 million in 1997–8 to 1.6 million in 2009–10 (Willetts, 2011) with 45 per cent of British school leavers attending university in the academic year 2011/12.[1] Also notable is the fact that today more women attend university than men: 49.2 per cent of female school-leavers, compared to 37.8 per cent of male school-leavers.[2]

The most noticeable change in American HE since the mid–1990s has been the increasing cost of university tuition fees. American students, already used to paying tuition fees within a marketised HE sector, now typically pay $45,000 for a four-year degree which rises to an average of $88,000 at a private university (Brzezinski, 2010). What has attracted public attention is not the fact of paying tuition fees, nor the total cost, so much as the rate of increase. Between 1988 and 2008 the average cost of a university degree rose by 375 per cent in comparison to a 127 per cent increase in median family income (Marcus, 2008). For three decades now university tuition costs have increased at more than double the rate of inflation.[3] This increase in fees has led to growing concerns about student loan debt, which increased by 24 per cent in the four years leading up to 2008.[4] There is national press coverage expressing anxiety at the issue of graduates 'defaulting' on student loan repayments: 8.8 per cent of borrowers who began repaying student loans in 2009 defaulted within two years, and for every borrower who defaults at least two more fall behind in payments. Default rates overall are currently the highest since 1997 (Lewin, 2011).

Throughout this period, the influence of the American HE system upon British politicians can be clearly seen. The lure of a marketised system and an assumption that such marketisation will automatically drive costs down and standards up has proved irresistible. However, it can also be seen that there are times when rhetorically, if not practically, it has been the other way round, and British influence can be detected in US policy documents. One difference between the two cultures is that British politicians make few explicit references to students as consumers or customers of HE; where such direct references do exist, they tend to be in speeches by government ministers or documents from the time when direct payment of tuition fees by students was first proposed, or to refer to behaviour other than fee-paying. For example, we can see that in the statement 'To become intelligent *customers* of an increasingly diverse provision, and to meet their own increasingly diverse needs, students need accessible information' (DfES, 2003b: 51 [my italics]) the word 'customer' refers not to the payment of fees but to selecting appropriate courses within an educational marketplace.

The language of educational consumption in Britain

It may be the case that in the UK there is political distaste for making explicit the status of students as consumers, as can be seen in this quotation from *Higher Ambitions*, the final HE strategy document published under the New Labour government, in 2009: 'The burden of financing higher education will need to be more equitably shared between employers, the tax payer, and individuals' (BIS, 2009: 22). Here, 'individuals' are counted as a group distinct from taxpayers (economically active adults) and employers.

In previous policy documents it is students who have been defined in opposition to taxpayers: 'Currently students who pay the full £1,100 fee are only contributing about a quarter of the average cost of their university teaching and education – the tax payer still pays the rest' (DfES, 2003: 87). Presumably the 'individuals' must be those who benefit from the higher education experience; that is, students, or their parents, either now or in the future. The use of the word 'individuals' in this context suggests a political reluctance to put a name to the 'beneficiaries' of HE and also reinforces the idea that the beneficiaries of HE are individuals; that is, that HE is a private good and that there is little public or social benefit to be gained from having a more highly educated population.

Also in 2009, the customer/consumer label was avoided by government ministers with a seemingly more forthright reference to students as 'fee-payers': 'Fee payers, business customers, and donors will expect to see a causal relationship between what they pay and outcomes attained' (BIS, 2009: 107). Placing students as 'fee-payers' alongside 'business customers' and 'donors' has the effect of making the three groups equivalent in status while the rest of the sentence makes explicit the consumer link between money and outcome. In the past, the education of students would have been considered the prime concern of the university, with business customers and donors of interest only to a small group of managers and administrators. On other occasions, the label 'client' is used to define students: 'As the most important clients of higher education, students' own assessments of the service they receive at university should be central to our judgement of the success of our higher education system' (BIS, 2009: 70). A 'client' can be considered as a person who uses professional services, or, in other words, a customer. What the term 'client' does not denote is any sense of equality, or potential equality in the relationship with academics. Clients are to be looked after and cared for but not necessarily challenged. What this statement also shows is that by placing students as 'clients' at the heart of the university, as opposed to students in a relationship to knowledge, the entire purpose of the university shifts to that of providing a satisfactory service; that is, flattering and appeasing students rather than intellectually challenging them through the rigorous pursuit of new knowledge.

Another emerging trend is for government ministers to identify a consumer attitude among students without accepting any responsibility for having helped to create such an outlook: 'There is now a perception that students are making increasing demands as "customers"; universities are now competing for students, especially international students'.[5] The noun 'perception' distances this view from the person who does the perceiving. The absence of explicit references to students as 'consumers' or 'customers' may of course indicate that it is taken for granted that they should be seen in this way. This certainly appears to be the case with *The Browne Review of Higher Education and Student Finance: Securing a Sustainable Future for Higher Education*, published by the Conservative-Liberal Democrat coalition government in 2010 (Browne, 2010). Here the word 'student' is used 664 times in just sixty pages. Yet ironically, it is this document more than any other so far published that argues the case for a higher education marketplace as a way to drive up quality and drive down costs. In America there is no such political introversion and politicians refer with candour to students as consumers.

By 1995, students in the UK were already well on the way to being constructed as consumers of HE. Maintenance grants were being replaced by student loans; the 'binary divide' between universities and polytechnics had been abolished and students had been officially labelled as the 'customers' of universities in the 1993 *Charter for Higher Education*. In 1997, shortly after the election of New Labour, Sir Ron Dearing's report of the National Committee of Inquiry into Higher Education was published. The *Dearing Report* did little to challenge the emerging status of students as consumers. In this report, Dearing sets out his 'vision of the learning society' and aimed to reassure universities that at the heart of this vision was 'the free standing institution [offering] teaching to the highest level in an environment of scholarship and independent enquiry'. However, Dearing continues: 'collectively and individually, these institutions are becoming even more central to the economic well being of the nation, localities and individuals' (Dearing, 1997: 1.22). This set the tone for an instrumental approach to HE which, although familiar to us already, goes qualitatively and quantitatively further than any previous government policy statement.

It is worth comparing Dearing's sense of purpose for universities with that of Robbins from 1963. Dearing indicates his perceived aims of HE as being:

- to inspire and enable individuals to develop their capabilities to the highest potential levels throughout life, so that they grow intellectually, are well-equipped for work, can contribute effectively to society and achieve personal fulfilment;

- to increase knowledge and understanding for their own sake and to foster their application to the benefit of the economy and society;

- to serve the needs of an adaptable, sustainable, knowledge-based economy at local, regional and national levels;

- to play a major role in shaping a democratic, civilised, inclusive society. (Dearing, 1997: 5.11)

Dearing contrasts these to the four (far more succinct) aims identified by the Robbins Committee:

- instruction in skills for employment;

- promoting the general powers of the mind;

- advancing learning;

- transmitting a common culture and common standards of citizenship. (Dearing, (1997: 5.7)

We can see that in 1963, of Robbins' four aims, only one relates directly to employment, whereas three are more concerned with learning for its own sake or for the creation of a socially cohesive society. By 1997 this emphasis has been completely reversed: three of Dearing's four stated aims make direct reference to work and the economy, and the only one that does not relate to work refers instead to the creation of an 'inclusive society'. It is worth noting that in 1997 New Labour most frequently defined 'social inclusion' in relation to employment (Williams, 2008).

When HE becomes so explicitly linked to employment, it is perhaps to be expected that Dearing should suggest that government and universities must 'encourage the student to see him/herself as an investor in receipt of a service, and to seek, as an investor, value for money and a good return from the investment' (Dearing, 1997: 22.19). This notion of HE as an investment is in many ways a logical conclusion of the discussion of human capital: the university has replaced on-the-job training and apprenticeships as the site for the development of this sought-after quality. Here we see where Dearing breaks with the established discourse of national economic advancement and instead focuses explicitly on private economic gains for which the student becomes an investor in his/her own stocks of human capital. The use of the word 'encourage' is notable because it suggests that at this time students do not automatically see themselves in this way. It was as a result of perceiving of HE as an investment that Dearing felt confident to suggest 'students should pay c. 25% of costs for HE through income contingent repayments' (Dearing, 1997: 20.79) through the introduction of 'income-contingent repayment of support for fees and living cost support' (Dearing, 1997: 20.78). According to Dearing's figures, this left the public to subsidise three-quarters of the cost of what was essentially to be seen as a private investment. This was justified by Dearing on the basis that there would be 'externalities' or 'spillovers' which would benefit non-graduates: 'so that gains to the economy as a whole exceed those accruing to the educated individuals' (Maskell and Robinson, 2002: 6).

Whereas it was previously considered that knowledge and science driving technological advancement would bring about economic development and subsequently employment for many in society, not just graduates, now the returns in terms of increased wealth and employment are seen to be accrued by graduates alone, and it is only 'spillovers' that benefit others in society.

Ultimately, the Labour government rejected many of Dearing's specific proposals on student finance. Significantly, however, it did share his beliefs about the general purpose of HE and its relationship to the economy and individual employability in a 'learning society'. As Education Secretary,

David Blunkett argued the need for Britain to become 'a leading knowledge based economy'. In this 'vision' of the economy, knowledge itself – rather than the material advances brought about through knowledge – is seen to be the driver of economic growth, and the people in possession of such knowledge are now considered the country's major national asset. This in turn led to the Labour government's objective that 'half of all young people benefit from higher education by the age of thirty' (Blunkett, 2000).

A further change proposed by Dearing, but not implemented, was the proposal that 'at least 60 per cent of total public funding to institutions [should occur] according to student choice by 2003' (Willetts, 2011b). This would have gone a long way down the line of increasing the marketisation of the HE sector at a much earlier date. The current British coalition government has gone back to the Dearing Report and found much evidence to support its current reforms. David Willetts, the current Minister of State for Universities and Science notes, perhaps with some relief: 'The Dearing Report also argued that "Government should shift the balance of funding, in a planned way, away from block grant towards a system in which funding follows the student". Even Lord Browne couldn't have put it better' (Willetts, 2011b).

The Teaching and Higher Education Act 1998, which was the legislation put in place following the Dearing Report, introduced from 1998 an 'up-front' tuition fee of £1,100 per year to be directly paid by students. This proved, initially at least, to be politically unpopular with the British electorate (Locke, 2011: 76). Paying tuition fees, however small and tokenistic the amount, became the most obvious symbol of the marketisation of HE. Tuition fees became the focus of public discontent and private disgruntlement, as students resented having to pay a fee that had not applied to those who had the good fortune to have been born a few months earlier. However, there was little challenge to the idea that HE was an investment in individual human capital and future employment prospects; this idea was accepted at the same time as the tuition fee was criticised.

From 1998, the issue of student debt began to be properly discussed for the first time. There was concern that debt was perceived by young people from socially disadvantaged groups as a barrier to entering university. Without challenging the notion of HE as a private investment, widening participation advocates argued for access to the increased human capital of this investment for more of the population. In accepting the fundamental premise that HE is a private investment, the argument that students are consumers of HE is all but won; the only issue for debate is who pays the bill.

A further way in which students were constructed as consumers by the 1998 Act was with the establishment of the Quality Assurance Agency (QAA). As students were expected to make a financial contribution to the cost of their education, the government's concern was to match this with enshrined rights and entitlements. Quality assurance is presented as a form of student empowerment as the QAA 'champions' the voice of students through regulating institutions' teaching and assessment practices. In the process of such regulation, the student experience inevitably becomes homogenised, as individual lecturers are expected to comply with demands for courses to be taught in credit-bearing modules with predetermined learning outcomes. The impact this has upon learning and teaching will be explored in Chapter Four. Perhaps more damaging is the assumption that lecturers cannot be trusted to provide students with an appropriate educational experience without outside regulation. Lecturers and students, presented as service users and service providers, appear pitted against each other with competing interests. There is a presumed need for an external regulating body to protect the interests of 'vulnerable' consumers against 'exploitative' academics.

Yet there is little evidence, anecdotal or otherwise, to suggest that academic standards have risen in British universities since the establishment of the QAA. Despite academics expressing disgruntlement at an increase in bureaucracy, there is relatively little criticism of the aims of the QAA, as the need for regulation is accepted and 'empowering' students is often considered a good thing.

The language of educational consumption in the USA

In America, 1998 brought the amendment and reauthorisation of the 1965 Higher Education Act. New initiatives were designed to:

- slash the student loan interest rate;
- help disadvantaged children prepare for college;
- improve teacher preparation and recruitment;
- promote high-quality distance education;
- create a new model for efficient government.[6]

These amendments reveal what was of most concern to the American government in relation to HE at this time. There was obviously anxiety that the cost of HE was escalating and that this was deterring children from less prosperous families from taking up university or college places. However, more money spent widening participation and cutting interest rates meant that savings had to be made elsewhere; and the fifth bullet point calls, in effect, for institutional cost-cutting. In addition, the 1998 amendments introduced Aid Elimination Provision, which aimed to prevent any student convicted of a crime related to drugs from receiving federal scholarships to fund their higher education.

This was about more than just cost-cutting: it formed one of a number of student drinking and drug use prevention efforts introduced with the 1998 amendments, suggesting that student behaviour, in particular the amount of time students spent socialising, was a national concern at this time. Recommendations were designed to 'address the problem of high-risk drinking on campus' (Epstein, 1999), in part through the appointment of a 'task force of stakeholders to fully examine student and academic life' at HE institutions. This could also imply that students were perceived to be more vulnerable than in previous generations and that institutions did not wish to accept legal responsibility for any behaviour considered as 'risky'.

The statement in the amendments asserting the need for institutions to 'maintain a safe and drug-free campus' (Epstein, 1999), despite having had no force in law, suggests that that the provision of a 'safe environment' has become a key preoccupation of potential students and their parents. University and college presidents are urged to 'Provide maximum opportunities for alcohol-free residence living and recreational and leisure activities' and 'eliminate alcoholic beverage-related sponsorship of on-campus events' (Epstein, 1999). A further addition to the 1998 amendments in section 952 authorises HEIs to 'disclose to parents and guardians violations of institutional policies or rules [...] governing the use or possession of alcohol or a controlled substance if the student is under 21' (Epstein, 1999). This means that parents will be told if their twenty-year-old son or daughter breaks an institutional rule (not a state or federal law) regarding drugs or alcohol. This suggests institutions are marketing themselves to the parents of prospective students on the basis that they provide a safe environment as part of the consumer experience. This perhaps heralds a return to the era of universities being *in loco parentis*, but rather than as a legal obligation now as a way of meeting the perceived demands of the institutions' customers – in this case, fee-paying parents. Such regulations are likely to be experienced as infantilising by students at an age when they are trying to establish their autonomy. This issue will be returned to in Chapter 6. Such regulations are also perhaps indicative of the beginnings of a more morally censorious climate on campus.

Perhaps the most significant development in higher education in the USA, heralded by the 1998 amendments, was the launch of the national GEAR UP initiative (Gaining Early Awareness and Readiness for Undergraduate Programs). GEAR UP is an early intervention and college awareness programme which aims to provide a guarantee of financial aid to enable disadvantaged children to take up a college place. However, the initiative goes much further than providing financial support, beginning work with children when they are in the Sixth Grade (11- and 12-year-olds) and 'seeks to provide long-term mentoring tutoring and other assistance to make the dream of college a reality'.[7] 'Other assistance' includes peer counselling, personal counselling, family counselling and home visits designed to improve parental involvement in the education of the child. What we have here is less about financial aid for a college place and more about full-scale intervention into the lives of young children and their families, based on the idea that 'disadvantaged' children are not merely materially disadvantaged but emotionally and psychologically disadvantaged through a parenting deficit (Williams, 2011b).

Such a programme can be seen as problematic when considered in conjunction with the measures to create safe campuses discussed above, because it begins to shift the purpose of HE away from knowledge and learning as an end in itself; away from knowledge for the national economy; away from individual employability and social mobility; and onto a more psychological terrain where the purpose of HE comes to be about nurturing the individual well-being and self-esteem of psychologically disadvantaged youngsters, within the context of a 'safe' environment (or at very least, in the absence of drugs and alcohol). Far from raising intellectual or material aspirations, this latest phase of higher education sees the university as a direct vehicle for therapeutic interventions into the lives of young people and their families.

Rising costs, changing expectations

In the UK in 2003, the White Paper *The Future of Higher Education* was published. At this time, 43 per cent of 18–30-year-olds in England entered HE (DfES, 2003a: 6). One aim of the policies set out in *The Future of Higher Education* was to harness 'knowledge to wealth creation' (DfES, 2003a: 6). Despite Dearing's assertion of the existence of a 'learning society' and 'knowledge economy', little had materially altered in the relationship between universities and industry. Thus the 2003 White Paper was used to try to engineer relationships between HE and business that did not already exist: 'less than one in five businesses taps into universities' skills and knowledge' (DfES, 2003a: 10).

The fact that these relationships did not exist perhaps calls into question the reality of a knowledge economy. Charles Clarke, then Secretary of State for Education and Skills, proclaimed: 'Higher education is a great national asset. Its contribution to the economic and social well-being of the nation is of vital importance' (DfES, 2003a: 14). The use of the word 'asset' suggests HE is seen as a commodity with an exchange value in the market. Here we can see continuing some state funding of universities is argued for on the basis of the impact HE has upon the national economy: 'So it is in the country's best interest to expand higher education' (DfES, 2003b: 20). It is notable that in 2003 it is felt that state funding of HE needs justifying in this way. The logical conclusion of these proposals is that there needs to be an increased role for employers in influencing the HE curriculum, to 'involve employers in the delivery of learning' (DfES, 2003b: 41). Although this is a justification for national funding for the whole sector, the arguments propounded indicate the purpose of HE for individuals.

As well as failing to bring about a knowledge economy, the 1998 Act had also failed in getting universities to operate according to a market. HE institutions were perceived to be under little pressure to respond to either the needs of business or the demands of students. One proposal to engineer this pressure upon institutions to respond to student demand was that student choice should be used to drive up quality, and that student choice should be encouraged through the publication of 'better information for students including a new annual student survey and publication of summaries of external examiners' reports' (DfES, 2003a: 11). This National Student Survey (NSS) was to be administered to final-year undergraduate students in the last month of their course, and focused upon levels of satisfaction with their student experience. This has led to the introduction of student satisfaction as a key driver of activity in the university and a mechanism for assessing teaching quality. The impact of this and its role in transforming students into consumers will be explored more fully in the following chapter.

In 2003 it was again proposed to make students pay an increased contribution to the cost of their tuition fees. This extra income into universities was necessary because, since the 1980s, the expansion of student numbers had not kept pace with institutional funding, leading to a steady decline in the income per student. This led to higher staff/student ratios which arguably resulted in an intensification of academic work and a poorer quality student experience. However, the political decision to fund this extra resource through student tuition fees rather than the public purse was further indicative of a desire to encourage the emerging market within HE. This is why it was proposed that the increased fees were no longer to be levied according to a 'flat rate', but that the best-performing institutions were to be able to charge most. In reality, however, all institutions set their fees at the ceiling of £3000. Such changes were motivated to students and their parents on the basis that 'Having a university education brings big benefits' (DfES, 2003a: 6), which reinforced the notion of HE as a private investment in human capital.

Political concern that increased tuition fees might lead to a decline in participation from more 'debt averse' students from financially disadvantaged backgrounds troubled Labour Party members, and the White Paper states the government's determination 'to ensure that access to higher education is broadened not narrowed' (DfES, 2003b: 4). Consequently, 2003 also brought the publication of the policy document *Widening Participation in Higher Education* and the creation of the regulatory body the Office For Fair Access (OFFA). This way, the government sought to negotiate the potentially contradictory aims of both increasing individual tuition fees and widening access to HE from under-represented groups. *Widening Participation in Higher Education*, however, focuses less upon providing financial subsidies than it does upon tackling a perceived lack of 'ambition' and 'aspiration' among non-participating youngsters. In this it pinpoints essentially psychological personality attributes as being the cause of young people's non-participation in higher education, a discourse reminiscent of the American focus upon counselling as part of the GEAR UP initiative.

The value of higher education

The Higher Education Act 2004 introduced variable tuition fees to English universities from 2006 (different funding mechanisms applied to universities in other parts of the UK). Students were able to fund tuition fees through taking out interest-subsidised loans with post-graduation income-contingent repayments. With the concept of income contingency came a message to potential students and universities that the level of tuition fees should be judged according to the theoretical 'likely benefits' (Locke, 2011: 77). This reinforces the notion that for students, HE is to be viewed not just an investment of time and energy but also a financial investment with a potential monetary return. In choosing a university to attend, the job of potential students is to weigh up the known cost against a hypothetical return.

In America in 2003 the Higher Education Act was again reauthorised, this time with two key amendments. The first was to continue expanding access to university and financial support for low- and middle-income students. The pressure group Alliance for Equity in Higher Education petitioned for funds for institutions attended mainly by minority groups, as well as more money directly to minority students. In this it was partly successful and some financial support was offered to minority graduate students and to specific institutions to enable them to keep pace with other universities and colleges.

The second main amendment to the Act in 2003 concerned the issue of accountability, which was becoming a growing concern in the light of rapidly increasing HE costs. There were calls for universities and colleges to be more financially accountable alongside demands for openness regarding students' educational progress. Newspaper reports from this time sought to expose universities which had spent money on questionable 'luxuries' unrelated to education (Weinberg, 2004). John Boehner, Chairman of the House Committee on Education and the Workforce, demanded to know: 'What are students, parents and tax-payers getting for their money?' He declared: 'Accountability is the hub of the education wheel [...] I want to explore how post-secondary institutions are accountable to students, parents and tax-payers' (Weinberg, 2004). A decade earlier, even in America, there would have been some surprise that knowledge, or learning was not the 'hub' of education.

It is a sign of how far HE has moved away from education to serve the needs of business and student-consumers that such a statement can be made. Boehner's words were echoed by those within the academy; Sharon Weinberg, Vice-Provost for Faculty Affairs at New York University, asked: 'How can we measure in a valid and reliable way, the success of our nation's investment in higher education? [...] What benchmarks should we use to signify the value of higher education?' (Weinberg, 2004). There is an assumption here that the value of education can be measured, and that the only issue is determining the correct tools to carry out this assessment of inherent worth. When education is conceived as more than just employability skills or a service to business, it is inherently unquantifiable. There is a risk that the focus on measuring the worth of education fundamentally alters that which is important about its content.

The focus on measuring returns is very much a logical conclusion of the assumption that HE is an investment. The idea that students should receive a specific return in terms of post-graduation income, or quantifiable achievements while in HE, adds to the idea of the student as consumer. Moreover, there is a danger that such demands for accountability will further erode the academic autonomy of HEIs, leading lecturers to teach a predetermined curriculum in a way that demonstrates the academic 'value added' most effectively. Educationally, this may lead to a focus on learnt facts or the demonstration of a narrow range of skills. Participation in a community of scholars and qualitative measures of educational development or intellectual engagement are more difficult to measure effectively.

In America in 2006, the Commission on the Future of Higher Education, led by the then Secretary of Education Margaret Spellings, published its report on the state of the nation's post-secondary schooling. In the past, such national reviews of the HE sector appeared to be primarily driven by a fear of international competitors overtaking the US both educationally and economically. In 2006 there was also anxiety that America had begun to take superiority in post-secondary education for granted and that quality in the sector had declined through lack of attention (Spellings, 2006: ix). However, the overwhelming sense from the *Spellings Report* is of a sector faced by an internal threat, a crisis from within the academy rather than a threat from abroad. A taste of this crisis is indicated by the statement: 'Over the past decade, literacy among college graduates has actually declined. Unacceptable numbers of college graduates enter the workforce without the skills employers say they need' (Spellings, 2006: x).

There is a palpable sense that, despite there being more students than ever before, more competition between institutions, higher student fees, and more state subsidy for HE, the expected returns are not only failing to materialise but educational standards are actually falling. There is a recognition that HE is operating within a 'consumer-driven environment', and that students care only about results (Spellings, 2006: xi). Yet rather than seeing this preoccupation with results rather than knowledge and learning as symptomatic of the decline in HE standards, Spellings welcomes it as a driver of accountability within the sector.

Spellings' aims for the American HE sector are reminiscent of Dearing in both style and substance:

- We want a world-class higher-education system that creates new knowledge, contributes to economic prosperity and global competitiveness, and empowers citizens;

- We want a system that is accessible to all Americans, throughout their lives;

- We want postsecondary institutions to provide high-quality instruction while improving their efficiency in order to be more affordable to the students, taxpayers, and donors who sustain them;

- We want a higher-education system that gives Americans the workplace skills they need to adapt to a rapidly changing economy;

- We want postsecondary institutions to adapt to a world altered by technology, changing demographics and globalization, in which the higher-education landscape includes new providers and new paradigms, from for-profit universities to distance learning. (Spellings, 2006: xi)

Essentially, Spellings indicates that the aim of HE in America is to contribute to the national economy through creating employable citizens in an inclusive and efficient way. The initial focus upon creating new knowledge is belied by social and economic instrumentalism. Spellings echoes the change that had already begun to appear in British HE policy documents regarding the relationship between HE and the economy.

Rather than higher education inspiring scientific and technological advances to drive forward economic development, Spellings presents the location of increased corporate profitability as within individuals: 'In tomorrow's world a nation's wealth will derive from its capacity to educate, attract, and retain citizens who are to able to work smarter and learn faster' (Spellings, 2006: xii). 'Proof' of profit emerging from within individuals is provided with statistics illustrating the higher wages achieved by graduates: 'Already, the median earnings of a U.S. worker with only a high school diploma are 37 percent less than those of a worker with a bachelor's degree' (Spellings, 2006: 1).

However, Spellings does not indicate exactly what is inherent in 'graduateness' that leads to increased profitability; it may be the case that education is used as a legitimate means of 'ranking' individuals according to the employment vacancies available: and that as more people attain higher level qualifications, or the number of job opportunities decreases, employers merely raise the entry threshold (Wolf, 2002: 35). French sociologist Pierre Bourdieu argued that academic devaluation such as this merely increases the significance of social and cultural capital (Bourdieu, 1990). Alternatively, certain degree courses, such as Law or Economics, or degrees obtained from a particular institution, such as Oxbridge or the Ivy League universities, become much more attractive as 'commodities' to student consumers looking to maximise the return on their investment.

The 'social mobility' trap

In assuming that graduates earn higher wages because of their enhanced human capital, it becomes logical for Spellings to argue that if there were more graduates the national economy would prosper, more people would earn higher wages, and America would become a more equal and socially just society. Spellings argues that HE should 'be the major route for new generations of Americans to achieve social mobility' (Spellings, 2006: 7). The unequal participation of all social groups in HE and the differential attainment of participants are indicated as both a cause and effect of social inequality which can be solved through HE (Spellings, 2006: 1). This explicit statement of education as the chief means of social mobility is quite new. In America especially, there had been a long-held assumption that the determined 'blue-collar' worker could, with sufficient effort, achieve prosperity. In the past education certainly had been used by individuals to achieve social mobility, and perhaps more frequently to confer higher social status upon the children of families made wealthy through trade and industry. However, social mobility was never the explicit purpose of post-secondary institutions.

Spellings' attempts to focus the HE sector towards the political goal of social mobility do not supersede the economic role previously given to universities and colleges. Rather it is the case that social mobility is considered to be brought about through the individualised economic function of HE. Spellings offers little explanation as to how universities should instigate such social engineering; there is only an assumption that it is the exchange value of the degree certificate in the post-graduation labour market that brings about social mobility. In this way the focus on social mobility serves to reinforce the construction of the student as consumer, as it emphasises the aim for students of obtaining a degree product rather than engaging in learning. Ironically, the liberal pursuit of knowledge for its own sake may well have brought about individual transformation in the past as individuals were encouraged to question everything they knew about the world. Today, when education is reduced to skills for employability this transformation is restricted to future job prospects.

In focusing upon social mobility, Spellings' huge success was to find a politically useful concept that had the power to bring together people from all sides of the political spectrum. As we will see, social mobility has been adopted with alacrity by both Labour and Conservative administrations in the UK. For some, a focus upon social mobility through education champions the values of individual hard work, determination and effort. It symbolises a person's ability to use their own resources and reject dependence on the state. Such a focus suggests that poor people have only themselves to blame for their poverty; they did not invest sufficiently in their stocks of human capital. For others, social mobility is about equal opportunities. Through opening up access to HE to more in society, it is presumed that there will be opportunity for socially disadvantaged groups to enter the professions and other high-paying jobs, and that this will lead to income redistribution and the creation of a more socially just society.

Such political consensus comes at a price – and in this case, the price to be paid is an erosion of the broader purpose of the academy in relation to the pursuit of knowledge, truth or scientific advance. There is a danger that a narrow focus upon social mobility may deny education a sense of purpose beyond employment prospects and income differentials. When universities downplay the importance of subject knowledge, students are left with little choice other than to position themselves as investors in their future employ-ability and consumers of an educational commodity. When academics no longer exhibit a desire to struggle intellectually with challenging new knowledge or, importantly, to inspire the next generation to seek to do this, students instead seek satisfaction in the short term. Seeking both future financial returns and short-term satisfaction consolidates the student experience into a consumer experience.

With all sides agreeing on the importance of social mobility, the only issue for debate within the *Spellings Report* is who should pay for HE. There is a sense that HE has become too expensive in return for poor overall returns (a point initially made in the 2003 Amendments) and greater efficiency is suggested: 'We propose a focused program of cost-cutting and productivity improvements in U.S. postsecondary institutions' (Spellings, 2006: 2). Ultimately this leads to calls for greater transparency over cost and results; colleges and universities are urged to publish more data on cost and 'student success outcomes' which Spellings proposes should be measured on a 'value-added' basis, taking into account students' academic entry level (Spellings, 2006: 4). There is an assumption that transparency of information will drive up competition and therefore efficiency within the HE sector, as potential students are able to make better informed choices.

More worrying to those concerned with academic standards is the assumption that what matters in relation to HE is not students' achievement but the progress they have made from their intellectual starting point. This means a student may in effect know very little upon completion of their degree but as long as this very little is more than they knew when they started they can be considered a success. This relativises the concept of academic achievement and further changes the aims of a university. No longer is there an expectation that the pursuit of knowledge is good for improving society's understanding of the world; rather, what is important is now the 'journey' individual students have undertaken. This transforms the role of the university away from the educational and towards the psychological. Rather than an expectation that students will engage with subject knowledge, there is instead a more therapeutic mission to encourage students to participate in projects of personal transformation.

Some of the recommendations of the Spellings Report were passed as legislation with the 2008 Higher Education Opportunity Act (HEOA). One key aim of the HEOA was to bring about the transparency within the sector that Spellings had called for. Although legislation was passed to bring about financial transparency, transparency in relation to student achievement remained voluntary. All institutions participating in national student aid programmes must now publish the estimated net price of a degree based on a student's individual circumstances. American universities have been criticised for advertising a high fee which, in reality, few students pay. Elise Miller, program director for the US Department of Education's Integrated Postsecondary Education Data System (IPEDS), argued the need to get beyond the 'the myth of sticker price'.[8]

Yet the logic of the HE sector market, urged into existence through successive legislation, means a high tuition fee is seen by customers as a proxy indicator of the value of the education universities offer: cheap degrees are considered unattractive, expensive degrees are considered reassuringly good quality and high in status. However, such a system requires prospective students to have the confidence and knowledge to negotiate such a system. Those without a family history of involvement in higher education may think the ticket price is what they actually have to pay.

'Social justice' through education and employment

In the UK there was still a Labour government in 2009, and universities were then part of the Department for Business, Innovation and Skills (BIS). Again, this represents more than just a bureaucratic name change; whereas the DfEE attempted to link education and employment in the popular imagination, making universities part of BIS indicated that they were not only integral to business but fundamentally considered a sector of business themselves with the claim that: 'UK universities' economic output is £59 billion a year, and amounts to 2.3 per cent of UK GDP' (BIS, 2009: 2). This is a major shift in the government's approach to the HE sector.

The publication in 2009 of *Higher Ambitions: The Future of Universities in a Knowledge Economy*, details how government will support universities to further develop their revenue generating potential. This primarily includes a focus upon 'STEM' (science, technology, engineering and mathematics) subjects and greater financial incentive upon universities to focus more effort on 'evolving economic challenges' (BIS, 2009: 8). However, beyond this, there seems to be relatively little vision as to how HE can drive the economy. Ultimately, practical proposals come down to individual students and their own employability and earnings potential: 'Even during the current global downturn, university graduates are more likely to be employed than non graduates; and graduates earn substantially more over their lifetime than non-graduates' (BIS, 2009: 2). This is similar to Spellings' claim that the source of economic profitability comes from graduates. Again, this narrowly financial focus appears to lead logically to broader social claims about the value of HE: universities are to be 'the providers of life chances for individuals in an environment where skills and the ability to apply those skills are essential preconditions for employment' (BIS, 2009: 3).

Having more graduates does not, in and of itself, create more employment opportunities; it merely raises the bar for everyone looking for a job and arguably, the people who suffer most are the non-graduates. The only solution proposed for this is to offer all young people advice on 'the availability of study and training options ... the choices pupils make can affect their later course options and life chances' (BIS, 2009: 6). Such discourse is by now familiar to us from the *Spellings Report*. The focus on individual opportunities means that *Higher Ambitions* places less emphasis on the connection between HE and the national economy, and links universities to employability in a very narrow sense of job training. The document states: 'All universities should be expected to demonstrate how their institution prepares its students for employment, including through training in modern workplace skills such as team working, business awareness, and communication skills. This information should help students choose courses that offer the greatest returns in terms of graduate opportunity' (BIS, 2009: 9). We have come a long way indeed from Newman and Arnold's arguments for liberal education.

Members of the Labour government were keen to appear to counteract this narrow instrumentalism with a broader purpose for the HE sector in relation to social justice. As Secretary of State for Business, Innovation and Skills, Peter Mandelson described universities as 'engines of social mobility' (Mandelson, 2009) and argued that there should be opportunities to participate in higher education for 'anyone who has the potential to benefit from it, regardless of background' (DfES, 2003b: 7). This exact metaphor was later employed by the Executive Vice-Chancellor of the University of California, Berkeley, who describes his institution as serving 'as an engine of upward social mobility for young Californians from low-income households' (Breslauer, 2011). Mandelson suggested that encouraging young people from socially and economically deprived backgrounds to take advantage of HE opportunities had become a question of social and economic justice as it helped equalise people's chances to obtain the degree product essential for individual social mobility: 'Because higher skills significantly influence life chances and earning potential, wider and fairer access to higher education is a question of basic social justice' (BIS, 2009: 8).

However, it can also be interpreted that once government has provided people with opportunities, the onus is firmly upon individual non-participants to conform and engage in education. Participation in education takes on the status of a moral imperative: a duty not just to one's self but to society more broadly. In this way, the act of participation in education is considered to be of value irrespective of knowledge content. The government's concept of social justice is brought about through the increased employment prospects and earnings potential offered by access to higher education, rather than anything intellectually or politically transformative.

'Social justice' was a key theme of the Labour government's policy from its election in 1997. One of Tony Blair's first acts as Prime Minister had been to establish the Social Exclusion Unit, with the aim of tackling social exclusion and promoting inclusion. Education was a fundamental part of this strategy. Education was thought to make people employable and therefore, through employment, people could be both included in mainstream society and financially better off. Education was thought to involve a particular social function which would cohere society, not through knowledge as with Matthew Arnold's vision, but through the participatory act of coming together in learning communities. Baroness Helena Kennedy, member of the House of Lords and New Labour policy advisor, argued for the importance of participation of post-compulsory education in 1997: 'The very process involves interaction between people; it is the means by which the values and wisdom of society are shared and transmitted across the generations' (Kennedy, 1997: 6). When removed from the focus on disciplinary subject knowledge, 'values and wisdom' are reduced to good citizenship and a psychological role in raising people's aspirations and levels of self-esteem.

Bill Rammell, as Minister of State for Innovation, Universities and Skills in 2008, explored the idea that HE is for creating better, more informed citizens:

> I think educational opportunity means people take in more information by and large. [...] You can have some incredibly well informed people with no qualifications whatsoever, however, they tend not to be the norm. By and large, the more educated people are, the broader the range of information out there that they have access to and therefore the better informed they are about the way decisions are taken and about things that they do that will impact upon their lives. If you do have that broader perspective [...] you are more likely to make decisions that are in your interests than would otherwise be the case.[9]

Here, the purpose of creating educated citizens comes to be seen in relation not to critical thought, but to enabling people to make 'better informed' decisions about their lives. There is a danger that this merely becomes another instrumental economic argument for education; that graduates save the nation money because they are, for example, less likely to smoke and more likely to exercise and eat a healthy diet. Rammell elaborates:

> It's not just about finance. Evidence does back up that getting a degree is still one of the assured routes to comfortable middle class security. But there's a whole range of other factors as to why people do it. You're much more likely to be in employment, you're much more likely to have an enjoyable job, you're much more likely to have a healthy lifestyle, and you're much more likely to engage in civic society.[10]

This statement begins to move HE away from a narrowly instrumental purpose in the sense of individual employability. However, this is not the same as education for its own sake. The argument that education plays a social role in relation to concepts such as a healthy lifestyle continues to endow HE with an instrumental purpose, simply one that happens to be more palatable to liberal sensibilities.

Choice and responsibility

Just one year later and after a change of government the Conservative and Liberal Democrat Coalition welcomed Lord Browne's independent review of HE funding and student finance: *Securing a Sustainable Future*. In some respects Browne's proposals were merely a continuation of what had gone before in terms of the rhetorical linking of HE to a knowledge economy. Statements such as: 'Higher education matters because it drives innovation and economic transformation. Higher education helps to produce economic growth, which in turn contributes to national prosperity' (Browne, 2010: 16) have become familiar over many years of HE policy. In some respects Browne implicitly acknowledges the failure of seeking economic growth through the skills of graduates: 'The higher education system does not produce the most effective mix of skills to meet business needs [...] 48% of employers were dissatisfied with the business awareness of the graduates they hired' (Browne, 2010: 25). Yet his conclusion is not that it is impossible to meet the needs of business through universities, but rather that there needs to be an even closer fit between the content of HE and the skills needs of the economy. This supports Labour's 2009 idea of universities as the location for job training. Browne's proposals and the coalition government's policy statements have been unpopular with liberal critics insofar as they have moved away from the emerging social purpose for HE identified by the Labour administration.

Where Browne goes further than Mandelson, and where he has attracted most criticism, is in his suggestion that students should be 'persuaded' to pay increased university tuition fees. Browne suggested there was a need to shift the balance of funding HE away from the national budget and onto individual students. This was partly because of a further increase in student numbers but also because in 'an age of austerity' with a government committed to cutting public spending, money spent on HE was considered a luxury the nation could ill afford. It was hard to justify public expenditure on what had been decreed 'a good investment' (Browne, 2010: 7) for individuals. However, no matter how directly linked to employment, education does not have a guaranteed return. As in the *Spellings Report*, Browne's solution to this problem is also an increased emphasis upon advice and guidance: 'Providing students with clearer information about employment outcomes will close the gap between the skills taught by the higher education system and what employers need' (Browne, 2010: 14).

Browne has a further reason for seeking greater transparency of information regarding different HE institutions and courses: the desire that students use information to exercise choice and in so doing to open up the HE market. He asserts: 'Students will be better informed about the range of options available to them. Their choices will shape the landscape of higher education' (Browne, 2010: 6). In the creation of a market Browne believes 'student choice will drive up quality' (Browne, 2010: 14), although there is little evidence that students would all agree upon a definition of quality in relation to HE or that they are able to assess quality in this way. Students may choose courses and institutions for a whole variety of reasons including location or the influence of friends, family and teachers. Students may associate quality with the likelihood of their being successful, in which case the less academically demanding the course the more popular it may appear. It can only be assumed that Browne's definition of quality education is one that gives the biggest return on investment or the most remunerative post-graduation employment. This is certainly not a definition of 'quality' that all within the academy would agree upon.

This focus on needing to provide students with increased information is continued in the latest government White Paper, *Higher Education: Students at the Heart of the System*. It is argued that students will be empowered through 'a new focus on student charters, student feedback and graduate outcomes' (BIS, 2011: 2). In addition, 'Universities will be expected to publish online summary reports of student surveys of lecture courses, aiding choice and stimulating competition between the best academics' (BIS, 2011: 6). It is assumed that the provision of all this information will ensure the operation of a market within the sector. As well as shifting spending away from the public purse the hope is that this market will mean that 'institutions will have to appeal to prospective students and be respected by employers. Putting financial power into the hands of learners makes student choice meaningful' (BIS, 2011: 5). Again, there is surely a risk that forcing universities to 'appeal' to students replaces a focus on the deferred gratification of gaining knowledge with the immediate gratification of the student experience; and replaces intellectual challenge with satisfaction. As in America, calls for greater transparency of information regarding the performance of particular institutions, courses and even individual lecturers are justified as necessary if the HE sector is to play a role in bringing about social mobility. It is assumed that a lack of information prevents working-class youngsters from applying to top ranking institutions.

In an attempt perhaps to counteract the focus on increased tuition fees, social mobility has been described as the primary role of the HE sector by the British government's Minister of State for Universities and Science, David Willetts. This is also made very clear in the 2011 White Paper and in the Government Strategy Document: *Opening Doors, Breaking Barriers: A strategy for social mobility*. The government's intention is that universities 'must take more responsibility for increasing social mobility' (BIS, 2011: 4). The imperative 'must' suggests universities are able to play this social role and just need urging to do so; 'responsibility' suggests there is a moral duty upon institutions to bring about this result.

By charging universities with the role of reaching out to disadvantaged youngsters to provide them with a service that will secure a future financial return (Willetts, 2011a), government has indeed made social mobility the domain of the HE sector. This individualised focus on social mobility is not the same as Labour's focus on social justice, although both serve to provide education with an instrumental sense of purpose that goes beyond the pursuit of knowledge.

The social mobility focus allows the government to increase the cost of university tuition fees payable by individual students and, at the same time, argue for widening participation in HE. Willetts expresses concern that 'the gap in participation rates between the most and least disadvantaged remains significant: the participation rate of the most advantaged 20 per cent of young people is 57 per cent compared with a participation rate of 19 per cent for the least advantaged 20 per cent of young people' (Willetts, 2011a). Indeed, the power for institutions to charge variable tuition fees is formally linked to their signing of Access Agreements to widen participation: 'No university will be allowed to raise its fees until it has an Access Agreement in place' (DfES, 2003: 87). The apparent contradiction between increasing tuition fees and widening participation in HE to under-represented groups is further resolved through a return to the notion of HE as an investment in individual human capital.

Through the promotion of social mobility, HE becomes explicitly linked to personal income as much as employability. As Business Secretary, Peter Mandelson argued that 'a university education remains the gateway to the professions and a ticket to higher lifetime earnings on average' (Mandelson,

2009). David Willetts agrees: 'Our research-intensive universities effectively staff the top of most of our leading professions. They are the places from which you get recruited into the best-paid jobs' (Willetts, 2011a). Various attempts have been made to calculate the financial gain from a university degree: in 2003 the figure was put at 50 per cent above average non-graduate earnings (DfES, 2003: 87) and Willetts calculates the graduate premium as 'still worth comfortably over £100,000 in today's money' (Willetts, 2011c). However, figures such as '50 per cent' or '£100,000' hide huge variations in earnings between graduates of different degree courses or institutions. Similarly, they take no account of the debts accrued by students or time spent out of the labour market in striving to achieve the graduate premium. More recently, research suggests that 'different subject areas are "worth" very different amounts in terms of lifetime earnings' (Zhu and Walker, 2011).

The logic of such economic arguments is that all students should study subjects such as law, economics and management, which are proven to give higher financial returns. A danger is that such financial generalisations create the idea that these sums are attainable to all irrespective of degree classification, course choice or institution. Furthermore, these claims promote the idea that this financial premium should be the motivation for higher level study. If HE is an investment, then it is only fair that it is made available to more of the population.

The statements by Mandelson and Willetts oversimplify a complex relationship, blurring effects of correlation and causation; and in doing so they promote the idea that the purpose of a university education is not knowledge, not intellectual challenge, not even especially skills, but job prospects and – even more specifically – income. This clearly stands in stark contrast to any idea that degree results should be connected to subject knowledge, accomplishment of particular skills, effort or application in a particular disciplinary area or that a degree should be studied for intellectual fulfilment.

Many academics, students, politicians and journalists on both sides of the Atlantic appear happy to agree that the main purpose of HE today is social mobility. Despite the current Deputy Prime Minister Nick Clegg being widely lambasted for reneging on pre-election promises not to raise university tuition fees, the then head of the National Union of Students, Aaron Porter, wrote of his belief that Clegg 'deserves a fair hearing on improving social mobility' (Porter, 2011). NUS President (2011/12) Liam Burns is candid in arguing that there is now a new motivation for HE:

> I think we should be honest about our priorities. At the end of the day, the point of the university has changed. If you look at when only 5% of the population went, that was all about knowledge, discovery, pushing boundaries, people talked about the crème de la crème. That's not the purpose of university now; it is about social mobility and people

changing their lives. The reality is you need that bit of paper to get into better jobs with greater earnings potential and influence. So we want as many people to get one as possible, at the expense of quality if necessary.[11]

Such a view of education being purely for social mobility 'at the expense of quality' may lead some students to adopt an instrumental approach to the pursuit of a degree certificate regardless of the extent of their intellectual engagement.

Conclusion

We can see that since the mid–1990s, the status of the student as a consumer of higher education is constructed primarily through policies focused on instrumentalism and satisfaction. The 'model' student-consumer wishes to possess a university degree in order to exchange it for social mobility in the post-graduation labour market. The same student seeks satisfaction in the process of gaining possession: a satisfactory student experience. Here we find many similarities with the reasoning behind widening participation. Arguments put forward to widen participation on the basis that it brings about social justice focus not upon the learning experience but upon the possession of a degree. The 'justice' is brought about through the exchange of the degree in the labour market. Students focus upon achieving a degree outcome rather than a challenging learning experience or engaging with intellectual content.

In purchasing the right to physical presence, students can remain focused upon instrumental outcomes and can avoid processes of intellectual struggle. Perhaps in response to this overt instrumentalism, a further seemingly more radical goal for higher education emerges in this period with a focus upon encouraging students to engage in projects of personal transformation. However, when transformation is removed from rigorous intellectual engagement with subject knowledge then the focus can only ever be the self. Reflection, without content, is necessarily limited and becomes reduced to psychological, or therapeutic, concerns with the self.

Endnotes

1 UK Statistics Authority (2011).

2 Higher Education Policy Institute (2011).

3 Marcus (2008).

4 The Project on Student Debt, http://projectonstudentdebt.org/files/File/Debt_Facts_and_Sources.pdf [accessed 20/07/12].

5 Students and Universities, The Eleventh Report to the Innovation, Universities, Science and Skills Committee 2009.

6 The White House (10/7/98) Office of the Press Secretary, Fact Sheet on Higher Education Amendments of 1998.

7 The White House (10/7/98) Office of the Press Secretary, Fact Sheet on Higher Education Amendments of 1998.

8 See http://www.studentaidservices.com/index.php/choosing-an-npc/the-requirement [accessed 20/07/12].

9 Interview with Joanna Williams.

10 Interview with Joanna Williams.

11 *The Herald* (13/2/11).

3

Constructing consumption

This chapter further explores the processes that construct students from both Britain and America as individuals who think and behave as consumers of higher education. This may begin long before students enter the university, as ideas regarding what it means to be a student and what university is for are presented by school teachers, careers advisers and guidance counsellors. Potential students are taught to 'shop around' in selecting a university; to look for the best product; to get value for money; and to find the course and institution that will best enhance their employability and lead to the greatest return on their investment of time and money.

Advice and guidance

In both the USA and the UK, school children, particularly those who do not have a family history of university attendance, may often gain their earliest understanding of what a university is and what it means to be a student from their experiences at school, in particular from careers advisers and guidance counsellors, mentors, or teaching staff acting in this role. In America this is most explicit with the GEAR UP initiative family interventions noted in the previous chapter. In the UK, the Labour government elected in 1997 made offering careers advice and guidance to young people a priority. As in America, much of this advice and guidance was focused upon encouraging young people, particularly those from social groups labelled 'disadvantaged', to stay on in education beyond the age of sixteen and ultimately to enter university.

In 2008, towards the end of Labour's period in office, the then Minister of State for Higher Education, Bill Rammell, spoke of the importance of ensuring that youngsters receive good quality advice and guidance:

> Too often people go, through no fault of their own, down the wrong path or fail to take a path at all because they weren't actually given the

right information and the right encouragement at the right time. I think
we've made huge progress over the past ten or eleven years educationally
and I actually think advice and guidance is one of the areas where we've
made least progress and we've got to get much better at it.[1]

There are a number of interesting assumptions made by Rammell here –
most obviously that there are 'right' and 'wrong' paths, or life courses. The
direction of one's life is a very personal decision, and to suggest someone
has taken the 'wrong path' is to make a value judgement upon the choices
that individual has made or the circumstances in which they have found
themselves. One can only imagine that Rammell thinks the right choice
– whatever the individual's desires or circumstances – is to remain in
education. Furthermore, Rammell assumes that if someone has made the
decision to leave education then this is because they have not received the
correct advice and guidance, not because the individual concerned has made
a choice that, for whatever reason, continuing in education is not for them.

In many ways it is surprising that Rammell suggests that the Labour
government has made least progress in the area of advice and guidance;
after all, this government was responsible for establishing the Connexions
Advice Service in 2000, designed as a 'one-stop shop' offering advice on
education, careers and personal issues to 13–19-year olds. In addition, the
Labour administration launched Aim Higher in 2004 as a national umbrella
group designed to bring together various widening participation initiatives
specifically aimed at recruiting youngsters from under-represented groups
into universities.

Although both Connexions and Aim Higher have been disbanded by the
current Conservative-Liberal Democrat coalition government; the concept of
formally encouraging continued participation in education remains central
to UK government policy. Widening participation is supported primarily
as a means of enabling individual social mobility. The British government's
most recent HE White Paper makes it clear that 'Potential students need high
quality advice and guidance to make informed decisions about whether higher
education is the right option for them and, if so, which route to take and
what subjects to study to prepare them for their desired course' (BIS, 2011:
56). While this may appear to suggest that students may be offered information on alternatives to entering university, the motivation for providing
such advice is made clear: 'Making sure that young people have access to high
quality, aspirational information, advice and guidance is an important part of
what schools can do to raise aspirations and support progression' (BIS, 2011:
56). The advice to be offered to youngsters is that there are different routes
into university and different courses available, and that not being 'academic'
should not be considered a barrier to entering a university. There is little to
suggest it is acceptable for youngsters to choose *not* to enter HE.

The image of higher education promoted to youngsters through such
websites will be influential in forming the attitudes and opinions they

have about what it means to be a student and the nature and purpose of a university. Although many prospective students will be most influenced by the attitudes and expectations of their parents, teachers and peers in deciding whether to go to university, official sources of advice provide a useful indicator of policy makers' views as to the purpose of higher education. Such sources encapsulate the message about university that one generation's political elite seeks to disseminate to youngsters in society. As such, the advice offered to young people indicates the nature of the HE sector they are about to encounter and in so doing manages their expectations and begins the process of constructing students as consumers.

Selling Higher Education

As discussed in the previous chapter, successive national governments in both the US and the UK have, for a number of years now, explored the purpose of higher education in predominantly instrumental terms (see Williams, 2008) and this is reflected in government-sponsored websites offering advice and support to 14 to 19-year-olds. One such website explores 'Options at 16' and asks potential students to consider the rhetorical question: 'What could higher education do for you?'[2] The student ('you') becomes the object of this sentence: the passive recipient of education which is 'done' for them and to them. Furthermore, by asking this particular question the expectation is framed that the purpose of entering HE is what individual benefits students may gain, not what they might have to offer the university or the more abstract world of knowledge or research. The answer provided on the website does little to challenge this notion: 'Higher education can open up new career options, and research shows that people with higher education qualifications typically earn more money than those without. They may also have more job security.'[3] School children being encouraged to apply to university can be left in little doubt – they are to be the passive beneficiaries of a process which can 'typically' lead to a job and more money.

A different page on the same website offers similar advice to older school pupils on 'the benefits of higher education'. Again, the heading assumes that there will be benefits, presumably of a material kind. Thus school students are told: 'Higher education could boost your career prospects and earning potential, while giving you a chance to immerse yourself in a subject that really interests you – and get involved in lots of other activities,'[4] and that: 'A higher education qualification can lead to increased earning potential, a wider range of opportunities and a more rewarding career. Many employers target graduates in their recruitment campaigns.' The most important point is reiterated for emphasis: 'And on average, graduates tend to earn substantially more than people with A levels who did not go to university. Projected over a working lifetime, the difference is something like £100,000 before tax at today's valuation.'[5]

Despite some initial acknowledgement that students may have some interest in the subject they are studying, the government's real perception of the benefit of HE emerges clearly: financial reward. So before they even complete application forms to enter university, school children receive the message that the aim of HE is to enable them to get a job and earn money. Education is presented to young people by government ministers as an essentially private investment from which material rewards can be accrued. Bill Rammell noted:

> If you want to adopt a generalisation, then for the vast majority of people, the greater the levels of qualifications that you gain, manifestly, the better your earnings potential becomes, and you see that right the way up. You certainly see it at degree level where the average graduate will earn £100,000 more net of tax than someone with just two A levels, over the course of their working life.[6]

That this view is shared by American politicians is made explicit by the US Secretary of Education (2012), Arne Duncan: 'We need to ensure that all students are able to access and enrol in quality programs that prepare them for well-paying jobs so they can enter the workforce and compete in our global marketplace.'[7]

Such statements reinforce the idea that for individual students, higher education is an investment of time and money that can be expected to yield a material reward. In America, the financial stakes are even higher; one estimate claims that college graduates can expect to earn $1.2 million more than high school graduates over their working life and that those with professional degrees can expect to earn $3.5 million more than high school dropouts. Even the most cautious estimate of average net return on investment was a lifetime gain in earnings of $627,239 (cited in Hess, 2011).

The relationship between qualifications and financial reward means that HE has come to be described as 'an entry ticket to the best paid employment' and 'a ticket to higher lifetime earnings' (Mandelson, 2009). The presentation of HE as a 'ticket' creates the impression that in attending university, students are accessing (perhaps purchasing) the 'graduate premium' (Smithers, 2007), irrespective of the extent of their engagement with the learning process. The metaphor of the 'ticket' suggests a very straightforward relationship between a degree certificate (not necessarily learning) and an entry route into well paid employment. In the context of increased tuition fees, government ministers have encouraged students to seek the degree that is most cost-effective at ensuring the greatest employ-ability prospects for the lowest initial outlay of both money and effort.

Value for money is assessed in terms of what the exchange value of the degree will be in the labour market; then Labour Higher Education Minister (2008–10) David Lammy suggested: 'The overwhelming majority of students from all backgrounds still consider the benefits of higher education to outweigh the costs' (Clark, 2009). Unsurprisingly perhaps, the idea of the Higher Education Minister that students should conduct a 'cost-benefit analysis' of their experiences in HE reinforces students' focus upon seeking value for money from a university experience. There is an assumption in both the British and American governments' demand for institutions to publish information to 'help students choose courses that offer the greatest returns in terms of graduate opportunities' (BIS, 2009: 13), that this is what students *should* be considering when making decisions in relation to university. Yet the fact that government ministers need to advise prospective students to interpret institutional data in this way indicates that value for money is not automatically considered a priority of this constituency.

This focus on value for money arises more directly as a result of university tuition fees which are the public focus of the shift to perceiving of students as consumers. It is perhaps only a logical consequence, many argue, that paying high levels of fees focuses the minds upon the outcome of achieving a degree certificate and the necessity of gaining post-graduation employment which is sufficiently remunerative to allow for the repaying of student loans. In 2010, the American College Board reported that annual costs for tuition and fees per individual student averaged $2,713 at two-year colleges; $7,605 at public four-year colleges for in-state students; $11,990 at public four-year schools for out-of-state students; and $27,293 for private four-year schools (Hess, 2011). These figures do not take account of accommodation and living expenses. A place at a University of California campus can easily now cost $13,000, or $31,000 including housing, given California's high costs.[8]

Average debt levels for American graduating seniors with student loans rose to $23,200 in 2008, a 24 per cent increase from $18,650 in 2004. In 2008 at public universities, average debt was $20,200, 20 per cent higher than in 2004, when the average was $16,850. At private non-profit universities, average debt was $27,650, 29 per cent higher than in 2004, when the average was $21,500. At private for-profit universities, average debt was $33,050, 23 per cent higher than in 2004, when the average was $26,850.[9]

Students who are expected to pay considerable sums of money for their university degree are likely to be a great deal more preoccupied with the worth of the end product and their future employability than students who left university comparatively debt-free a generation earlier (Golan, 2011). One recent American graduate comments on how the need to secure remunerative employment influenced her choice of course: 'I was going to college to advance my career, to get an opportunity to actually control my economic future. So I didn't go to college and major in anthropology and philosophy. I went to college and I majored in business because I wanted to get a job' (Zernike, 2009).

Sam, a British psychology undergraduate aged 21, comments on the impact fee-paying has upon the learning process:

I don't know anyone who's doing university purely to learn [...] I was originally more like I'm really interested in Psychology but seeing all the numbers on paper I have to gear myself towards money a bit more than towards passion. It definitely changes your focus.[10]

Here Sam suggests that although his initial motivation to study had been driven by an interest in the subject, his focus altered upon arrival at university, and the start of receiving student loan statements and tuition fees bills in particular. Melissa, a 19-year-old Psychology student, says of her chosen subject:

I've found it interesting since I was about fifteen or something and it's been a long time and I just, everything about it, all the studies. Just learning about people that's what I find the interesting bit. I think my motivation isn't so much about money but it's at the back of my mind, I'm always conscious about that. It's more the fact that I want to learn.[11]

What Melissa expresses here is a conflicting view between being motivated to study to reap a financial reward on her investment or because she is interested in the subject and 'wants to learn'. British academics Mike Molesworth, Elizabeth Nixon and Richard Scullion note that 'Students have long experienced a tension between approaching learning with an internal drive for self-development and the external requirement to have the right amount and type of knowledge to operate in the market' (Molesworth, Nixon and Scullion, 2009: 281). What has changed in more recent years is that this personal tension of motivation has been replaced by a vocal public endorsement for students to focus solely upon developing private employability skills.

The main thing students need to secure future employability is a degree certificate irrespective of the amount of learning that may or may not have taken place. For some students the desire for a degree certificate replaces the desire to be a student of their chosen subject. Educational instrumentalism belies pretension to the pursuit of knowledge for its own sake and instead creates students who do what it takes to succeed 'where succeed is defined in terms of graduation' (Potts, 2005: 62). As a result, the aim for many students becomes obtaining the outcome (a degree) rather than a full engagement with the learning process.

In American universities promoting the employability of future graduates is financially incentivised because if students do not earn sufficient income to pay back their student loans and default (fail to meet the repayment schedule) institutions can be penalised. In an era of national economic insecurity the risk of students failing to gain remunerative employment and defaulting on their loans is increased. Institutions with excessive default rates can lose their eligibility to federal student aid programs. This will affect recruitment as it makes the institutions less attractive to prospective students and more likely that students in need of state scholarships to fund their higher education will look elsewhere. At most American institutions, courses that fail to recruit sufficient numbers to be financially viable are swiftly closed.

In 2011, five institutions were subject to sanctions for high cohort default rates (defined as over 25 per cent defaulting for three consecutive years; over 40 per cent in the latest year, or both). In the financial year 2009 the national student loan cohort default rate rose to 8.8 per cent, up from 7.0 per cent in the previous year. More than 320,000 students of the 2009 graduating cohort defaulted on their loans.[12] In the light of such steep penalties American universities are under more pressure to ensure their students gain employment post-graduation and to make degrees more about job training than academic content. For example, Thomas College, a liberal arts school in Maine, markets itself as 'Home of the Guaranteed Job!' (Zernike, 2010).

There are now only a few suggestions that higher education is of intrinsic importance, worth financing or encouraging simply because education is important in its own terms. For example, Bill Rammell argues:

Do I think there's an intrinsic case for education? Yes, of course I do. There is absolutely a case for the pure, personal benefit from education but that's not the only gain that you get from education and of course, in addition to that, we do want skills for employability [...] I think it's about fulfilling both functions. I don't think you can pursue one narrow set of objectives only.[13]

Here we see that Rammell tries to make the case for education for its own sake but confuses this firstly with 'personal benefit' which is not quite the same and as a result falls back upon a familiar discourse of 'skills for employability'. He reveals his belief that pursuing education for its own sake would be 'a narrow set of objectives'. In 2003 then Labour Education Secretary Charles Clarke famously proclaimed education for its own sake to be 'a bit dodgy' and argued that students need 'a relationship with the workplace.'[14]

Unsurprisingly, students do to some extent take on board the message behind government-sanctioned advice and begin to think of HE in a direct relationship to their future career plans and job prospects. This is not caused solely by the payment of tuition fees: fee-paying simply reinforces the relationship. As Sarah, a 19-year-old Sports Science student, explains:

For me it does seem like a lot of money to pay but I'm hoping that afterwards I'm going to get my money's worth, kind of thing. When I graduate it's going to be worth it and I'm going to get a job that can help pay it back. If I came out of it without getting a job that could pay off the fees then I'd be worried.[15]

For Sarah, her degree will be 'worth it' if she gets a job that can enable her to repay the tuition fees. This says little about the perceived intrinsic reward of the learning process or the desire to gain knowledge in a particular subject area.

The views of Sandra, a 41-year-old mature student and single mother, who explores the need for a degree to enhance her employment prospects, are also typical of those who have bought into the concept of education as an investment:

> The whole point of me actually doing a degree was so that I've hopefully got better earnings potential anyway. I could probably do the same job without a degree; maybe social care, probationary officer. You can still do that on training but your earnings potential with a degree is higher.[16]

Sandra sums up her attitude towards paying tuition fees by saying at several points in our interview: 'It's an investment'. In such ways, students' attitudes reflect the universities' persistent emphasis on their employability records. Before students even step foot inside a university, their horizons have been narrowed to encourage them to approach HE as an investment of time and money; tuition fees simply enhance awareness of the financial nature of the transaction between student and university. Some commentators suggest that students should, in effect, stop moaning and that high levels of debt are not a necessary prerequisite for obtaining a degree: 'There are much cheaper HE options such as community colleges. If a student does choose to pay the huge cost of an elite institution, given their lifetime earnings it is only right that they bear some of the cost' (Hess, 2011). There is a danger with this argument that academic liberal education comes to be perceived as the preserve of the wealthy whilst non-traditional students focus upon employability in order to repay debt. This is ironic given that the focus upon social mobility arises out of efforts to promote widening participation to precisely such non-traditional students.

Critics of recent government policies note that fee paying may create a 'two-tier system' whereby students who have to borrow heavily to get a degree are very likely to choose courses of study that offer the best chance of securing lucrative post-graduation income; in subjects such as Business, Law or Economics. At the same time the pursuit of less vocational subjects, such as within the humanities, will become a luxury only available for the wealthy. This is borne out by Carole Leathwood and Paul O'Connell's study of 'new' or 'non-traditional' students in higher education: 'It appeared that the emphasis needed to be on studying modules that are likely to have currency in the job market and prepare them for work. Non-vocational modules and those studied purely for pleasure were, perhaps, considered too great a risk' (Leathwood and O'Connell, 2003: 611). Similar divisions have also been noted over choice of institution by the American National Center for Education Statistics which estimates that just 26 per cent of the nation's 19.1 million two- and four-year college students are attending private institutions (cited in Hess, 2011). Again this reflects a divisive system where not just choice of course but also choice of institution will be driven by financial motives and attitude to future debt.

It remains the case that, in general, the students who secure professional careers and highly remunerative work tend to be students who have attended the highest-ranking institutions and studied the most academic courses. For example, in the UK top journalists are far more likely to have studied English literature or politics at a Russell Group[17] university, than to have studied a vocational course in media studies at a lower-ranking institution. A further irony of the British 'pseudo-market' with its cap on tuition fees is that nearly all institutions are proposing to charge fees at or near the cap, for all courses. In a positional market, to charge much less than the cap appears to send an adverse message to potential students about the quality of the institution. Despite huge variations in the potential 'value' of university degrees, there will be minimal differences in the fees students are charged. Non-traditional students who lack the social and cultural capital necessary to negotiate their way through the complex hierarchies of institutions and courses could potentially pay high levels of fees for degrees which carry little weight in the employment market.

Information as currency

In order to counteract the emergence of a two-tier system, the British government wants institutions to publish information to create a transparency regarding fees, university experience and graduate employment just as the Spellings Report from the USA suggested in 2006. In a somewhat circular argument, potential students are considered to need greater information in order to make choices within a marketised HE sector; and yet such information is considered crucial to the establishment and operation of a market in the first place. Britain appears to be following the American emphasis upon accountability and transparency. Institutions get caught up in a 'morality of visibility' (Morley, 2003: 84) where not exercising complete transparency appears, at best, as if the university has something to hide, and at worst as putting under-represented students at a further disadvantage in choosing a university.

In America, demands as to the nature of information that universities should provide to the public in general and prospective students in particular have considerably broadened over the past decade. The state of Texas, for example, requires public universities and colleges to 'post syllabi on-line, with detailed information about classroom assignments, as well as faculty members' curricula vitae, student evaluations, and department budgets. The information must be no more than three clicks away from the college's home page' (Brown, 2010). In addition universities and colleges are expected to provide detailed crime statistics on or near their campuses, so that potential students and their parents can assess the crime risk (Coughlan, 2011).

The British government's proposals are remarkably similar, in instructing institutions to provide 'information on the proportion of time spent in different learning and teaching activities. This should be supported by links to more detailed information at module level, for example about the time engaged in different types of teaching and learning activities including lectures' (BIS, 2011: 26). This information is to be presented to students in the form of 'Key Information Sets' (KIS) so that students can make quick and easy comparisons between institutions. Former NUS President Aaron Porter supports this push for transparency and accountability, claiming that 'the idea of giving key information to applicants is a great leap forward' (Coughlan, 2011). The idea is that KIS will enable students to compare HE institutions in the same way they would compare the market when choosing to purchase any other product or service.

The assumption that HE institutions can be compared in the same way as car insurance or personal computers indicates what is wrong with this focus on increased information being made available to prospective students. KIS cannot possibly provide an objective measure of the quality of education a student may be likely to receive: the nature of education makes such a measurement impossible. Nor can KIS provide a measure of the intellectual challenge students will face. Instead KIS is to primarily contain information about 'graduate employment prospects [...] employment and earnings outcomes' (BIS, 2011: 6). It will also include measurable information such as contact hours, assessment methods and pass rates. The provision of this quantifiable information commodifies education into a tangible service, and the direct link between education and employment presented in such information further encourages prospective students to adopt an instrumental approach to their education, constructing students as consumers before they arrive at university. Qualitative information on the individually transformative nature of the learning experience, and the intellectual challenge and encouragement to work hard within the chosen academic discipline, is impossible to include within a KIS framework.

There is a perception that such detailed information is needed to protect supposedly 'vulnerable' students in the light of institutions that adopt sophisticated marketing techniques. Increased tuition costs represent a shift in institutional funding sources. In California, following years of tuition fee increases far steeper than the average at American public universities, students now contribute more to universities through the payment of tuition fees than the state gives to the universities in funding. This means that universities must now work to attract students through the marketing of a desirable product, not for profit or additional extras, but for their core funding. Aaron

Porter welcomes KIS on the basis that it adds substance to universities' marketing efforts:

> There has been an explosion of marketing from universities in recent years, with claims about the facilities on offer [...] Students are enticed by the flowery marketing-speak. But there are surprisingly few details about the curriculum and the learning experience. The open days are stage-managed events and there are stories about flowers being planted specially and buildings repainted. (Coughlan, 2011)

There is a risk that this portrays students and potential students as uniquely vulnerable, further infantilising youngsters at the start of their adult life. Such a claim also portrays universities and lecturers as corrupt salesmen, eroding the trust between students and lecturers before students enter university.

The advice and guidance youngsters receive at school and the information provided by universities and colleges thus encourages prospective students to consider themselves as consumers before they even enter HE. Knowledge and learning is not presented as an intellectually exciting journey so much as a commodity that can be measured in contact hours, assessment methods and certificates. The impact this has upon the way students approach subject knowledge and learning will be explored in the next chapter.

Customer service and student charters

In America, if students were in any doubt that they were HE customers before entering university or college, it is again made very clear to them upon arrival, where lecturers are frequently positioned as service-providers. At Prince George's Community College in Maryland, near Washington DC, a customer service campaign saw all members of staff issued with identity badges bearing the slogan 'Have we served you well?' (Marcus, 2011). At Fort Valley State University in Georgia, employees are required to hang in their offices a framed sign that reads 'FVSU is Committed to Friendly and Efficient Service' as part of a drive 'to compete in a truly customer-driven manner'.[18] Although students at Idaho State University may not see their lecturers wearing badges or displaying such signs, they may be reassured to learn that there is a customer care initiative offering cash prizes to employees for exceptional customer service.[19] Cornell University in New York similarly offers a six-week course for faculty and staff called 'Customer Service – The Cornell Way' which teaches that 'a university has customers, internal and external, just like other organisations. Every interaction between alumni, a prospective or current student, faculty or staff provides the opportunity for our university to make a favourable and lasting impression'.[20]

Such examples may appear brash to British sensibilities. But there is surely only a difference of degree between 'Have we served you well?' badges and the many posters on display in corridors and teaching rooms at Canterbury Christ Church University in the UK telling students, 'You Said: We Did'. The message is exactly the same: students are consumers and what consumers demand they shall receive. The role of the lecturer is merely to serve the consumer well.

The making explicit of consumer status upon arrival at university in the UK is reinforced through the use of charters which provide students and potential students with a written statement detailing 'the mutual expectations of universities and students' (BIS, 2011: 33). Charters provide an indication of the level of service students can expect to receive and what they will be expected to do in return. In 2010 the British Conservative-Liberal Democrat coalition government established the Student Charter Group, comprising representatives of universities and other higher education institutions as well as student representatives, to explore current practice in the use of student charters and other student agreements. The use of charters was recommended by the Final Report of the Student Charter Group in January 2011, and has since been positively endorsed in the government's 2012 HE policy document. Yet as noted in Chapter 1, the idea of charters for universities and students is not new; the publication in 1993 of the Department for Education's *Charter for Higher Education* played an important role in the emerging concept of students as consumers.

In 1993, it was intended that one document would cover the whole of the HE sector – rather than each institution having its own charter, as is expected to be the case today. The 1993 Charter was aimed at potential students and aimed to inform them how 'all these bodies [local and national government offices] respond to the needs of the *customers* of higher education'.[21] This is one of the first official government documents to describe students as 'customers'. The word 'customer' appears three times in the 'Short Introduction' to the Charter, signed by the then Secretary of State, and recurs throughout the slim pamphlet. Students are considered to be the customers of the university alongside members of the local community, employers who purchase the human capital of graduates, and businesses which purchase the results of research. The 1993 Charter formally decrees the role of a university to be delivering a service to these groups of people. It was also in 1993 that the importance of value for money in the pursuit of higher education was established; the Charter 'points out the steps that are being taken to secure better value for money, for example in the way that quality will affect funding for courses.'[22] The Charter perhaps provides an indication as to how value for money should be evaluated: 'You should know in advance how your course should be taught and assessed.'[23] There is no explanation given as to why students are expected to know this and what use they are to make of such knowledge.

The aim of the 1993 Charter is to make 'everyone more aware of what is provided for the large amount of public money that goes into higher education.'[24] This established the idea of HE as having a *quid pro quo* relationship with the public: 'This Charter explains the standards of service that students, employers and the general public can expect from universities and colleges and other bodies involved in higher education in England.'[25] Public money was spent on higher education in expectation of a clear return. This *quid pro quo* was also to form the basis of the relationship between universities and students: 'Customers of universities and colleges also have responsibilities and the Charter reminds you of some of them.'[26] Students had the 'right' to receive a service but, in turn, were expected to exercise responsibility with the public money spent on them.

The shift since 1993 has been away from seeing this process as an expenditure of public money and an expected public return, to an expenditure of private money (in the form of tuition fees) with an expected private return. When public money was spent on university students the return was expected to be in the form of a better-qualified, internationally more competitive labour force which would enable the creation of jobs for non-graduates. Similarly, university graduates would meet the public need for key social roles such as doctors, dentists and teachers; and higher earners would be expected to contribute more to the economy in the form of taxation. Now, university is presented in terms of a private role and the returns of higher wages, greater job security and satisfaction are expected to be experienced solely by the individuals who have gained the degree product.

If we accept at face value the statement of the 1993 Student Charter – that students are 'customers' of the university – then the most recent introduction of charters could be seen as an example of students exercising their 'consumer rights' in making demands of the institutions which receive their tuition fees. However, there is little to suggest that this is the case. Instead the latest demand for universities to have charters appears to come from central government. In most recent HE policy documents and speeches, the government's Department for Business, Innovation and Skills is presented as an arbitrator or 'consumer rights champion' defending the interests of vulnerable students against universities intent upon taking their money in return for a poor quality service through 'giving students power to hold universities to account'.[27]

That such an attempt at championing the rights of the student consumer should take the form of institutional charters is indicative of the fact that HE is now considered to be a private contractual investment between individuals and institutions. In addition, a number of universities, such as the University of Sheffield, already had some form of formal student contract in place designed to 'clarify the terms' of the relationship between student and university (Newman, 2007). Previous forms of student contract were largely disciplinary in nature and designed to set out the behavioural expectations of students, sometimes even down to what the institution considered to be appropriate forms of dress. In America, such contracts are often used to set out the academic expectations of students who receive bursaries or scholarships to cover a proportion of their tuition fees. Such contracts may stipulate that students fulfil attendance requirements as well as maintaining marks above a certain grade point average.

British institutional charters, as proposed by the *Student Charter Group Final Report,* are a move away from disciplinary contracts and are a response to the major funding changes facing the sector which, it is acknowledged, 'have the potential to alter the relationship between universities and students.'[28] It is unclear from this whether 'altered relationships' are to be welcomed or discouraged. There appears to be an assumption that through formally setting out mutual rights and responsibilities, such changed relationships can be managed in a way that is positive for students. The 2011 government HE policy document, *Students at the Heart of the System,* emphasises the need for all institutions to have charters that provide: 'Information for students when they are starting a course – and during the course – so they know what they can expect and what is expected of them',[29] in order to 'establish clear mutual expectations, and help monitor the student experience and how relationships are working' (BIS, 2011: 4). There is an assumption that students and academics cannot be trusted to negotiate such relationships for themselves but need some form of contract for mutual protection.

In setting out 'mutual expectations', charters go beyond mere provision of information and begin to establish a more contractual relationship whereby students' expectations as to the level of service they will receive are matched by expectations upon them to behave in a particular way, for example by attending lectures and seminars regularly or meeting assessment deadlines. Vice-chancellors have to negotiate with student leaders at each university and college the standards that they will promise to deliver to undergraduate and postgraduate students. Ironically, one obvious effect of this is that it removes individual academics from negotiating relationships with their students; the presumed interests of a generic student are 'set in opposition to the vested interests of knave-like academics' (Sabri, 2010).

For many HE institutions, charters take the form of bullet-point lists of things that 'We Will' and 'You Will', under headings such as 'Academic Achievement', 'Learning and Teaching', and 'Extra Curricular Activities'. One such charter at use in a British HEI, Bishop Grosseteste University College Lincoln, begins: 'The Charter outlines the responsibilities the University College has to its students. It also outlines what responsibilities Bishop Grosseteste expects its students to fulfil, in relation to the institution, its staff, other students and partner organisations with which they work'.[30] This further serves to reinforce the idea of HE as a *quid pro quo* relationship, with students encouraged to expect a guaranteed outcome in return for particular behaviours. In so doing it reduces studying to behavioural acts such as attendance at lectures and meeting deadlines. The extent of intellectual engagement becomes irrelevant to the behaviour demonstrated.

As we have seen, there is actually an awareness that much of the learning that takes place in HE is through 'relationships': relationships between fellow students and between students and academics. This point is recognised by the Student Charter Group which emphasises 'the importance of partnership between staff and students'.[31] The aim is that 'in focusing on rights and responsibilities, students will understand the need to develop effective working relationships'.[32] The main issue here is whether 'effective working relationships' can be managed, monitored and regulated in this way. It may be the case that the more relationships between staff and students of a university become regulated and formalised through such instruments as charters, the less effective they are at bringing about learning. Spontaneity, passion and enthusiasm are all difficult qualities to legislate into existence. In the 2011 British government HE policy document it is argued that charters are needed as: 'They will help to provide consistency of practice across different subject areas' (BIS, 2011: 33). The implication is that inconsistency of practice is detrimental to students. This makes no allowance for different lecturers to adopt idiosyncratic approaches according to their personality or, perhaps more significantly, their academic discipline. Forcing lecturers to teach in line with consistent practice is unlikely to engender passion.

It is acknowledged by the British government that 'to pursue higher education is to belong to a learning community and that the experience will be most enriching when it is based on a partnership between staff and students'.[33] Yet this sentence begins: 'Charters should emphasise that [...]', which reveals the government's belief that learning communities and effective relationships can be imposed upon institutions. In practice this means that students are told, under the heading of 'Academic Achievement' that their lecturers will: 'Assess your work in a way which is fair, efficient, professional and externally verified'.[34] The fact of telling students that their work will be dealt with in such a way calls into question the professionalism of lecturers: students may assume automatically that their lecturers will be professional, and such a written statement may raise, for the first time, the suggestion that they might not be.

Students are told to 'Ensure you are dedicated and conscientious in your studies' and 'Take responsibility for your own independent learning.'[35] Again, one might reasonably expect that any student embarking upon a degree and with some interest in their subject will show some commitment to their studies. The formal statement of such a principle may make students question whether their interest is shared by their peers. In terms of learning and teaching, students are told they will 'Participate actively in seminars, workshops and other group work.'[36] Such statements suggest the physical busy-ness of students is rated more highly than their intellectual efforts.

Charters appear to be about regulating staff just as much, if not more, than students. The *Final Report of the Student Charter Group* makes this clear: 'Charters can be especially useful when introduced during induction for students but also for new members of staff.'[37] Indeed, this is how charters have been reported in the media: 'University charters to tell lecturers they must do better,' proclaimed a headline in a British broadsheet newspaper.[38] The use of charters as a tool to publicly discipline wayward lecturers further constructs academics as service providers unable to exercise academic judgement or to establish individual relationships with their students. Perhaps worse than this is the creation of a pervasive sense that lecturers and students have opposing interests that require external regulation. Staff-student liaison committees become reduced to customer complaint forums with lecturers pushed to assume a defence of their practice. A consequence of assuming conflict of interest between client and service provider is that it 'inexorably erodes the relationship of trust between teacher and student on which academic enterprise is founded' (Furedi, 2009: 2). The charter becomes a service-level agreement which British academic Louise Morley describes as being part of a low-trust/high-risk culture (Morley, 2003: 84). There is little opposition to charters from lecturers, as they are seen as 'empowering' students with better consumer information and arguing against student empowerment or the dominance of the student voice is akin to challenging the 'sacralisation of the consumer' (Sabri, 2011: 658). Yet the notion that as young adults students can be 'empowered' by an institution, rather than taking control of their own educational experience, reduces the concept of empowerment to a service level agreement (Morley, 2003: 84).

Bishop Grosseteste Charter contains sections outlining students' responsibilities in relation to extra-curricular activities and health and safety, which suggests the institution is increasing its sphere of influence over the lives of its students away from the more traditional academic concerns of a university and into students' whole lives. For example, the charter states under the heading of Health and Safety: 'You will: Not engage in activities which put you or others at risk'.[39] The definition of an activity which puts 'you or others at risk' could be very broad. Driving, forming relationships or drinking alcohol could all be classed as potentially risky activities and yet are arguably part of the experience of becoming an adult. Some may even argue that learning itself is an inherently risky activity, in that it can challenge everything students hold to be true about the world. British Professor of Education Dennis Hayes argues that putting students at the heart of the university can mean that the passing on of knowledge is no longer the aim of lecturers: 'And if that student is seen as a vulnerable person whose vulnerability is your concern, then it is difficult to challenge their thoughts and beliefs' (quoted in Reisz, 2011). Although universities have not held a legal position of *in loco parentis* towards their students since the legal age of majority was lowered to 18 in 1969, it appears through charters that universities regain a formal responsibility for non-academic areas of a student's life.

The existence of charters contractualises a relationship which should be about intellectual collaboration, collaboration inherently dependent upon a degree of free will. Furthermore there is a danger that in telling students what they should expect to 'get' in advance removes all elements of social, emotional or intellectual risk from their HE experience. Yet it is precisely such risk which is necessary for intellectual and personal growth; that is, for real learning to take place. The use of charters serves further to construct students as consumers in a way that is detrimental to positive learning relationships between students and lecturers. In focusing upon the *quid pro quo* of what you 'get' in return for what you pay through the framework of formal rights and responsibilities, the use of charters may serve to formalise the status of students as consumers in a way that fee-paying alone does not.

Conclusions

Few of today's students arrive at university as a 'tabula rasa'. The idea of a university degree as a ticket for future employability with an expected financial rate of return is promoted heavily to students from the moment they first begin to consider higher education. This concept of the degree 'ticket' separates out academic success from intellectual effort. Rather than focus on being a student or immersing themselves in a favourite subject, students instead focus upon having a degree. The tuition fee invoice reinforces the idea that students are entitled to a university degree in exchange for their time and money.

Rather than universities challenging the idea that a degree is an entitlement, institutions instead strengthen this notion. The provision of quantifiable information on contact hours, assessment patterns and employment prospects suggests students are correct to perceive of a degree as a product. Lecturers are presented as service providers whose aim is to do what the customer demands ('you said: we did'). Lecturers who fail to provide students with a good enough service are brought into line through the use of charters which set out the exact nature of a student's entitlement. Universities contractualise relationships between student and academic: instead of students embarking upon an exciting intellectual journey and negotiating entry into learning communities with lecturers as mentors or guides, they merely seek to claim their entitlement. The impact this has upon students' learning and relationship to subject knowledge is the focus of the next chapter.

Endnotes

1 Interview with Joanna Williams (22/04/08).

2 http://www.direct.gov.uk/en/EducationAndLearning/14To19/OptionsAt16/ DG_066261 [accessed 20/07/12].

3 Ibid.

4 http://www.direct.gov.uk/en/EducationAndLearning/UniversityAndHigher
   Education/WhyGoToUniversityOrCollege/DG_4016998 [accessed 20/07/12]

5 Ibid.

6 Interview with Joanna Williams.

7 Press Release, US Department of Education (12/09/11).

8 Staff Reporter (10/09/11) in *The Economist*.

9 'Debt Facts and Sources', The Project on Student Debt.

10 Interview with Joanna Williams. The names of all student interviewees have
   been changed.

11 Interview with Joanna Williams.

12 Press Release, US Department of Education, (12/09/11).

13 Interview with Joanna Williams.

14 In BBC News (31/01/03).

15 Interview with Joanna Williams.

16 Interview with Joanna Williams.

17 The name given to a group of twenty leading UK universities.

18 Marcus (2011).

19 Marcus (2011).

20 Marcus (2011).

21 Student Charter 1993 1 – my emphasis.

22 Student Charter 1993.

23 Student Charter 1993, 12.

24 Student Charter 1993, 1.

25 Student Charter 1993, 2.

26 Student Charter 1993, 2.

27 Student Charter Group Final Report (January 2011) 37.

28 Student Charter Group Final Report (January 2011) 4.

29 BIS (2011), 3.

30 Bishop Grosseteste University College Lincoln Student Charter, August 2010.

31 Student Charter Group Final Report (January 2011), 7.

32 Student Charter Group Final Report (January 2011), 7.

33 BIS (2011), 33.

34 Bishop Grosseteste University College Lincoln Student Charter, August 2010.

35 Ibid.

36 Ibid.

37 Student Charter Group Final Report (January 2011), 7.

38 *The Times* (01/04/10).

39 Bishop Grosseteste University College Lincoln Student Charter, August 2010.

4

Teaching consumption and consuming learning

The previous chapter explored the processes involved in constructing students as consumers prior to entering a university. When students arrive at university, the view that they are to think of themselves as consumers is often made explicit for the first time, as Sarah, a 19-year-old sociology student explains:

> One time we had a questionnaire come round, they said to us 'you as customers of the university' and we're thinking we're not customers; we don't come in every day and buy stuff from you. But although I guess in a sense we are because we're giving them our money for something in return.[1]

This chapter considers the impact of being constructed as a consumer upon students' attitudes to learning, knowledge, and their relationship with lecturers once at university. Institutional approaches, especially forms of pedagogy – that is, the ways in which students are taught – seem to determine the adoption or rejection of a consumer identity above and beyond the actual payment of fees. In this chapter I look at what, if anything, has changed in the way students approach learning and relate to subject knowledge at university.

Whilst on the surface students may appear to attend lectures and sit exams as they have done for generations, this may mask a shift in emphasis for some students away from intellectual engagement with content matter towards a focus upon doing what is necessary to gain the particular degree classification needed for post-graduation employment. Lecturers may seek to challenge such attitudes or may find that the increase in student numbers and demands upon their time makes acquiescence easier. Alternatively, as consumers, students may feel more engaged with their learning as they perceive themselves empowered to influence the content of the curriculum and the pedagogical approaches adopted by their lecturers as they complete satisfaction surveys and sit on feedback committees. However, in some instances, lecturers' compliance with the demand for student satisfaction may run counter to a focus upon intellectual challenge and may result in some students feeling alienated from academic disciplinary communities.

Learning instrumentalism

One impact of students considering themselves, and being considered by others, as consumers of higher education is that they adopt an increasingly instrumental approach to university, and seek a degree 'product' rather than a learning experience. It has been suggested that today's students seek to *have* a degree rather than to *be* learners (Molesworth, Nixon and Scullion, 2009). This move from 'being' to 'having' represents an intellectual shift from engagement to passivity, with some students seeking satisfaction in the fulfilment of their rights as opposed to a struggle with theoretical content. This is represented in newspapers: 'The problem with treating students as consumers, many observed, was that it gave them the impression they had rights but no responsibilities. "They think that because they are paying they should be awarded a 2.1 without making any effort," was a repeated complaint' (Clare, 2006). The very fact that the British government needs to state: 'A good student is not simply a consumer of other people's knowledge, but will actively draw on all the resources that a good university or college can offer to learn as much as they can' (BIS, 2011: 33) suggests that this is not something that students are doing as a matter of course. Instead of intellectual engagement, students are encouraged to seek value for money in their degree purchase.

Once students are told that value for money is what they should expect to receive, they understandably seek to obtain it. Sarah, for example, speaks of needing to 'get her money's worth'. Donna Bowater, a Warwick University graduate, says she found herself with few contact hours and she 'admitted to one fellow student in my first year that the free time allowed me to participate in extracurricular societies that students with a heavier workload could not. He replied: "But at least they're getting their money's worth"' (Hurst and Sugden, 2010).

In trying to make sense of judging value for money in relation to education, many students equate 'value for money' with contact time with teaching staff (more being necessarily better, although this may run contrary to the promotion of more independent learners). Sarah relates a conversation she had with a friend:

I think a lot of people would shoot me for saying this but paying tuition fees makes people respect what they get a lot more. It's their money and it's like when my friend said she didn't want to go to her lecture I was like, well, when you go home find out how much it is and divide that by how many lectures you have and every hour that you miss it's that much money you've thrown down the drain. You wouldn't go and pay for a meal and then not turn up and not have it.[2]

Here we can see how the lecture or seminar 'hour' becomes the tangible commodity some students perceive they are purchasing in exchange for their tuition fees. Alex Harlow, aged 20, a first-year History student at Leeds University in the UK, said: 'Six and a half hours a week for £3,500 a year – it's extortionate. I went to a fee-paying school and it cost more than university but the stuff you got out of it and the extracurricular things made it much better value' (Hurst and Sugden, 2010).

There is an assumption here that the more contact time students have the better quality of education they must be receiving. However, this just does not always hold true for higher education and measuring hours becomes a crude substitute for the quality of educational experience. One reason for this is that not all contact hours are used in the same way. Educationally, it is difficult to equate an hour spent in a one-to-one tutorial based on material both student and lecturer have considered in advance, with an hour spent in a workshop alongside fifteen, or fifty, other students. More contact hours may certainly keep undergraduates busy, and may well provide students with useful structured learning opportunities, but this will be a qualitatively different educational experience to an undergraduate course that puts emphasis on fewer, more intense meetings with lecturers.

At one time, British students spoke of 'reading' for a degree, which summed up the notion that they were immersed in their subject in a way that went beyond just turning up for classes, rather reflecting a broader intellectual engagement with the disciplinary community. The concept of 'reading' for a degree also suggests an aspiration towards intellectual independence and an ability to work within the discipline in a less structured way than at school. In this lies the expectation that university students will move beyond being taught facts and will begin to create new knowledge for themselves. Even if this is an unrealistic goal for some first-year undergraduates, the move away from a school-like structured timetable at least encapsulates the aspiration that HE students should strive towards intellectual independence and that they are capable of gaining this by the final year of their undergraduate studies.

The demand that students should receive more 'hours' in exchange for their money is reported in mainstream newspapers: 'There have [...] been well-publicised cases recently about students complaining about the amount of "contact" with teachers, and the more publicity there is about this, the better' (Bekhradnia, 2009). Such discussions over contact hours are frequently used to portray lecturers as 'work-shy', or, at best, too preoccupied with their own research to give time to the needs of undergraduate students. This presents academics and students as being on opposite 'sides' and with opposing interests. Such a presumed opposition is not conducive to the creation of scholarly communities.

Similarly, for some students, value for money may come to be equated with academic success: if students are rated highly by their lecturers they consider themselves to be gaining value for money; if they receive low marks, they are less likely to think that this is the case. The majority of formal complaints lodged against British universities each year are about assessment and final degree marks (Garner, 2009). Similarly, in America, there is a reported increase in the number of students lodging complaints to their institution about the Grade Point Average (GPA) they have been awarded (Dinkins, 2009). Such an equation of value for money with academic success is perhaps only the logical conclusion of a degree being considered of extrinsic worth for its purchase in the labour market rather than of intrinsic worth for the learning experience gained in completion. By this reasoning, 'value for money' could be assured for all students by eroding academic judgement and awarding everyone high marks irrespective of actual achievement levels.

Fortunately for university lecturers, many students are only too aware that education is more than just a sum of its quantifiable parts, and that value for money is impossible to assess. American Social Science student, Dave, shows far more wisdom than most government ministers when he argues: 'You have got to make sure you are getting value for money. But then, you don't know what value for money is, do you? Because you have not had the experience before and probably never will again. So this is it, this is university' (Cooper, 2004: 6). Even if it were possible to measure value for money in relation to education, students would need to be in possession of all the specific knowledge content to be covered and have a comparative overview of a range of pedagogic approaches; as students they are not likely to have this knowledge.

In order to help students make sense of value for money the government requires all universities to publish statistics relating to the post-graduation employment of past cohorts of students, as discussed in the previous chapter. In order to be able to report successful employment outcomes, all current students are expected to focus on future employability. This may take the form of encouraging all students to attend careers workshops where they will be offered advice on completing application forms, interview techniques, and presenting the skills gained from their degree course in a way that is attractive to potential employers.

Perhaps the most obvious appearance of this focus upon employability is the growing prevalence of vocational courses which aim to offer students a direct route into specific careers. For some careers, such as nursing, the formal requirement to hold a degree level qualification is relatively new. Other courses, such as journalism, perhaps take the place of the 'on-the-job' training that would have occurred a generation ago.

Less obvious, although arguably more insidious, is the impact an institutional focus upon employability has had upon students studying for all courses, and not just in specifically vocational areas. Students are encouraged to think of even non-vocational subjects strategically from an early stage in their time at university in terms of future job prospects. Similarly, lecturing staff are expected to indicate the employability skills students are developing as they proceed through degree courses and students are often expected to log new employability skills in portfolios that can be shown to future employers. Whilst this may appear logical in relation to some particular vocational courses which train students for very specific careers, such as sport and leisure management, nursing or physiotherapy, it appears a more cumbersome addition to philosophy, English literature and classics courses. In the UK, the Higher Education Academy (HEA) runs conferences for philosophy lecturers to discuss how they will best promote student employability within their subject area.[3] At Exeter University, students can opt for a Humanities in the Workplace module.[4]

Also at Exeter University, course structure is presented in terms of employability. For example, humanities seminars are no longer justified on the basis that they provide the most disciplinary appropriate format for the discussion of texts, but rather that they allow students opportunities to gain skills of working in small groups, giving presentations and managing discussions.[5] The form of the seminar comes to replace the content as the most significant learning experience. What becomes important for the students is not immersion in an interesting and relevant discussion but a reflection upon the skills gained. In America, degree programmes regularly have their curriculum 'upgraded' to ensure maximum relevance to students' demands and the perceived needs of employers.

In part this relentless promotion of employability is due to a need for institutions to appear attractive to new students by demonstrating the employment success of previous cohorts; and in part it is a (perhaps presumed) response to student demand in the face of mounting debt levels. However, the employability agenda must also be recognised as resulting from a collective loss of faith in the ability of academics to argue the case for purely academic subjects in their own terms. When lecturers are unable to defend teaching philosophy, for example, as an end in itself, instrumental ends are brought in to justify the existence of the subject within the HE curriculum. If studying an academic subject cannot be justified because it makes an essential contribution to our collective understanding of what it means to be human and the nature of the society we live in, it must instead justify its existence in the more mundane sphere of employability.

Flexible consumption

A further institutional change that has occurred in response to students paying fees and becoming perceived as consumers of higher education is the assumption that even full-time 'traditional' students will be combining study with employment and will therefore need to be able to achieve a degree in the most time-efficient way possible. Individual universities implement policies designed to promote flexible learning as well as 'credit systems which make it possible to break off and start again without having to repeat learning' (DfES, 2003b: 68). The premise is that studying will be just one activity amongst many in a person's life and something to be accommodated around other commitments.

Policy documents declare the need for institutions to 'expand new types of higher education programmes that widen opportunities for flexible study for young people and adults and reflect the reality of the modern working lives' (BIS, 2009: 11). Although combining study with work and family commitments is undoubtedly a reality of today's mass HE system and socio-economic climate, the declaration that study should be part-time and flexible as a norm perhaps reinforces the notion that it is the degree product that is to be obtained rather than an immersion in the learning experience. Such moves towards flexible study echo the demands from government and student consumers for 'efficient teaching methods' that provide 'maximum outcomes for minimal effort' (Molesworth, Nixon and Scullion, 2009: 283). This focus on efficient teaching, and its appraisal through the National Student Survey (NSS), encourages lecturers to 'give students what they need to pass' rather than encouraging a more critical engagement with subject content.[6]

If the priority for students, many institutions suggest, is placed upon getting a degree over and above any learning processes students may undertake, it is no longer considered important for students to have a coherent learning experience, drawing together disciplinary specific knowledge to create a greater understanding of the world from the perspective of their subject. Instead institutions promote a modular approach to degree programmes which reflects the combined demands for teaching efficiently and flexibly. Under a modular approach, subject knowledge is constructed into small units and students pick and choose modules to suit their learning styles, preferred assessment methods, timetabling convenience, and favourite lecturers. Modules are then individually assessed. But education is about more than just the sum of its parts. Just as driving, for example, cannot be taught through passing separate tests on using gears, steering and braking, similarly a person cannot be truly educated through passing separate modules on disparate content. Through modular course design, students come to expect 'knowledge served up in easily digestible bite-sized chunks' (Trout, 1997: 50).

Being educated requires an ability to relate new knowledge to things learned previously. British academics Rajani Naidoo and Ian Jamieson suggest that 'close and sustained engagement with the content and internal structure of a discipline may be crucial in enabling students to master complex conceptual structures and modes of analysis for purposes of knowledge creation' (Naidoo and Jamieson, 2005: 275). Yet the nature of course modularisation is to hinder rather than to promote this sustained engagement. A modularised structure promotes the idea that higher education is about collecting module credits, almost like stamp collecting, rather than developing a coherent intellectual overview of the chosen discipline.

Instrumental rather than educational aims, presented to students in the form of distinct modules, may encourage students to adopt a 'shallow' or 'surface' approach to learning (Prosser and Trigwell, 1999: 14) which focuses upon the need to meet course requirements and fulfil assessment criteria in a way that circumvents the need for a deeper understanding of content. The modularisation of courses, and the demand that students demonstrate having met particular learning outcomes in order to pass module assessments, assumes that learning is something which can be tangibly demonstrated in a particular format and within a given time scale. Modules have prescribed 'learning outcomes' which inform the student in advance what they will have learnt upon completion of the module, or, in other words, the areas in which the student must demonstrate competence in order to pass. The need to meet learning outcomes encourages students to approach assessment tasks in a formulaic manner, providing sufficient information to demonstrate accomplishment without necessarily having developed a deep understanding of intellectual content.

A modularised approach to higher education and the lack of an intellectually coherent disciplinary overview for many students can prevent students from feeling a sense of belonging to a learning community. This can make the students appear alienated from the institutions they attend, a situation exacerbated by the fact that over the past couple of decades British universities have been financially incentivised to expand student numbers without a corresponding increase in the number of teaching staff. Mature student Sandra explains: 'You just feel like a face really in the lectures, you're not anything else because the lectures are about 200 to 300 people,' and this is echoed by Sam, who proclaims: 'I didn't expect it to be that big though. It's huge; it's two hundred-plus people in there.'[7] This sense of being 'just a face' is reinforced by being with different groups of students depending upon the modules chosen and not developing disciplinary knowledge alongside peers undertaking the same intellectual journey. Louise Morley notes that in a mass higher education system, 'there is a danger that students are not constructed as scholars to be handcrafted, but rather as entities in an industrial or manufacturing battery process' (Morley, 2003: 82).

That students adopt an instrumental approach to their learning may seem to place students and lecturers in opposition to one another, as lecturers may seek to promote 'deep' learning and understanding of their subjects to students who are 'persistently instrumental and assessment orientated' (Molesworth, Nixon and Scullion, 2009: 282). This may suggest that relationships between academics and students could become 'disaggregated with each party invested with distinct, if not opposing interests' (Naidoo and Jamieson, 2005: 271). Having purchased access to a knowledge commodity that carries a particular exchange value in the labour market, a sense of engaging in intellectual struggle may seem anathema to some students.

This has led some to comment that there is a growing tendency for students to seek to 'have ideas, or skills as if they were possessions that can be bought, rather than to know ideas as ways of seeing the world and skills as ways of acting' (Molesworth, Nixon and Scullion, 2009: 280). Others concur that students demonstrate 'a loss of responsibility for their learning and a resistance to engaging in education as a process rather than a purchasable product that is simply appropriated' (Naidoo and Jamieson, 2005: 273). This consumer model of higher education 'encourages the student to forego honesty and free inquiry in favour of "doing what it takes" to "succeed" where "succeed" is defined in terms of graduation and the receiving of a college degree' (Potts, 2005: 62). This can have the perverse effect of preventing students from gaining a sense of intellectual satisfaction, or enjoyment, from their course at precisely the time when universities most seek to have demonstrably satisfied students. Satisfaction comes to be found in arenas away from the academic, hence institutional obsession with the 'student experience', rather than student learning or just teaching.

Learning, participating or attending?

Tom, a 20-year-old sociology student, suggests that some students draw a distinction between work and leisure – and as a result of seeing studying as work they initially stop enjoying it and then lose interest in the subject matter:

> A lot of people don't do reading because they're not enjoying it [...] people are viewing it as work. It seems like people are looking at the exercises and the essays and all that as work versus something to help you learn. [...] It's a lot more easy to open the book if you are interested versus 'Oh well, I have to learn this so I can write a paper on it.'[8]

It is perhaps because university is now viewed through the prism of consumption that students interpret intellectual work as a chore rather than an opportunity to engage with something that interests them. If the student is a consumer, and the consumer expects a service in return for payment, then traditional notions of 'hard work, responsibility, and standards of excellence' are rendered meaningless (Trout, 1997: 50).

Yet students themselves express dissatisfaction with this model of education. Patrick, a geology student, explores one problem he perceives with students adopting an instrumental approach to their education:

> I think that if you're a consumer then you'll learn only what you need to know [...] and everyone will learn the same thing. People are not being encouraged to think for themselves. That's where all the great ideas come from. Not just academic ideas; join societies, start something very, very new [...] I mean, those are things, if you were a consumer, you wouldn't have that chance, you'd just be thinking this is what we need, this is how to do it.[9]

What emerges here is a sense of a distinction between a consumer's experience of university linked to doing that which is necessary to graduate in the most efficient way possible, and a somewhat idealised student experience of 'great ideas' and 'doing something new'.

The existence of students such as Patrick may serve to remind government ministers of alternative models to higher education to those based upon skills for employability. Gemma Tumelty, who was President of the UK NUS in 2006, asked: 'What about learning for learning's sake? [...] What about expanding your mind? It's not just about looking for a course that will get you on the career ladder.'[10] There is evidence to suggest that many students are looking for intellectual challenge in their courses (Ashwin, Abbas and McLean, 2011). Melissa, a nineteen-year-old psychology student, explores her motivations for choosing her course in terms of her interest in the subject:

> Well, I did it for A level as well and it was one of my favourite subjects. I've always kind of been a people watcher and I like sort of looking at behaviours and things and it just seemed like the right course to do for me [...] I just really thought it would be interesting.[11]

Many students genuinely want to be excited by someone passionate about their discipline, not counting contact hours and ticking off assessment methods. Yet some lecturers do not promote passion and interest in their subject but rather focus upon telling students what they 'need' to know rather than what students might find interesting to know. In a seemingly vicious circle, it is the assumption that students are consumers and only interested in securing a degree product and the pedagogic practice associated with this belief that confirms those ideas by students.

Tom explains further:

[...] we have this study skills thing, they're more oriented on this is how you have to do the essay; this is how you are supposed to study; this is how you do referencing. And the PhD student that's teaching us there seems more of like, you just have to write these papers because you have to write papers, versus you have to write in this format for your learning. They're coming and being like, 'Oh you have to work through a ton of studies, you're probably not going to like it.' So this in turn makes people think they're not going to like it and they don't like it because of that. You're not focussing on learning from the essay but you're focusing on just getting it done and turning it in and getting a 2.1 or a first.[12]

Tom suggests that the attitude of some of his tutors that students won't enjoy the course and just want to be taught the most efficient way of getting the outcome they need is 'caught' by the students. So, although tutors are not addressing students as customers, the attitudes they demonstrate, rather than the language they use, can engender a degree of instrumentalism.

Melissa defends her lecturers:

They just treat you like a student, they don't think you're paying fees. I think they treat you as a student, they want to teach you, they want you to learn, so I don't really feel like they're kind of thinking you've paid good money for this, I'd better make it good.[13]

But then continues:

Obviously it helps to have an interest in the subject [...] but they [lecturers] kind of treat you, like sort of say, you need to know this, not rather, you probably want to know this, it's, kind of, I've not heard anyone say this would be really interesting, but instead they say you should look at this and you need to know this.[14]

This view is shared by Sam who expresses the hope that:

They'll realise like when we do optional modules and stuff it's because we actually want to do them.[15]

And Patrick suggests:

Each lecturer, they're all fantastically informed so I think they enjoy, you know, spreading the subject and teaching people about it but in terms of how to write the essay they just say this is what you need to do to get a 2.1.[16]

This might indicate a separation between the attitudes of lecturers teaching subject content (which they are free to enthuse about) and the attitudes which emerge when discussing assessment and course outcomes (more routine and procedural and subject to more formal university regulations). The focus lecturers place on outcomes – for example, the aim of writing an essay in such a way as to secure a particular grade or classification, monitoring attendance and monitoring participation in seminar groups in quantitative rather than qualitative terms – places emphasis upon extrinsic rewards and sanctions rather than an intrinsic sense of reward gained from having mastered new knowledge. The immediate gratification of an essay mark replaces the longer-term intellectual satisfaction of drawing connections between distinct areas of knowledge. Such a presumed need for rewards and sanctions is 'based on a one-dimensional view of human nature', note Naidoo and Jamieson (2005: 274), and lecturers holding such views may risk substituting pedagogic commitment for enthusing a new generation of students with a passion for their subject.

Furthermore, an extrinsic focus upon the 'reward' of a particular grade or qualification in return for following particular rules disincentivises intellectual risk-taking on behalf of both students and lecturers. In order for students to feel able to take intellectual risks there needs to be freedom for both lecturers and students to move beyond the behaviourist restraints of learning outcomes. Lecturers need to be able to assess students' work on the basis of its intrinsic quality rather than simply boxes ticked. Students cannot trust that intellectual risk-taking will be rewarded when they consistently receive messages to work in a particular way to secure a certain grade. Institutional procedures similarly discourage lecturers from allowing students the freedom to pursue an idiosyncratic approach to their learning. Instead, Naidoo and Jamieson suggest the 'requirement to comply with extensive external monitoring procedures may encourage them to opt for "safe teaching" which is locked into a transmission mode where pre-specified content can be passed on to the student and assessed in a conventional form' (2005: 275).

A problem with this lack of intellectual freedom is that 'good' hard-working, well-motivated students, in attempting to engage with knowledge, become more entrenched in forms of consumption. Francesca, a nineteen-year-old Sports Science student, comes closest to voicing this attitude when she expresses her exasperation with fellow students:

My lectures have never been cancelled. My classmates always think I wish my lecturer was missing now, I don't have any mood to learn anything. You pay for it, why don't you want it? If you don't want to study don't come then. We will have a class in the future and there will be knowledge that no one else will give me and if I don't attend I will lose.[17]

The use of the noun 'knowledge' in this quotation is interesting: in this context knowledge becomes an almost tangible object, something which can be 'given', presumably by a powerful teacher-figure, as 'no one else' can give this knowledge. The role of the student is to 'attend' the class and receive the knowledge: this results in a passive relationship to learning. The consequence of not attending is to 'lose' – another interesting choice of word which suggests that learning is somehow a competition or a race, that there are a finite number of winners who can possess the knowledge product. This suggests learning is 'an individual possession, something which can be acquired' (Harrison, 2004: 176).

When knowledge is viewed as an object to be possessed, and one which can give you a competitive advantage over others, then the idea of paying for such an object becomes entirely rational: 'it deserves so much money,' continues Francesca. There is a danger that the politicians' insistence upon a focus on outcomes rather than processes will enhance the creation of a consumer mentality along with the belief that students should seek to obtain a degree product rather than participate in lengthy periods of study. This stands in contrast to the idea that HE should be considered as a 'relationship' between lecturers and students, a relationship which is 'structured by purpose and content' (Biesta, 2009).

Instead of being structured through purpose and content the relationship between students and lecturers comes to be structured around skills, or perhaps more accurately, values and attitudes. This again, is often linked to employability. Rammell argues:

> The skills that having a really good degree can give to you are not purely vocational, it's actually much more about analytical skills, it's about confidence, and it's about the ability to solve problems. It's about an ability to communicate with people. Now, do all of those come directly from higher education? Was I sat down and taught all of those as part of the programme? No, I wasn't. They were a by-product that wouldn't have come about without me studying in the way I did.[18]

There is a blurring here between skills and values, and between what should be taught and what may be just a by-product of the university experience. What is only tacitly acknowledged here is that the by-product comes from rigorous intellectual engagement in subject matter.

The skills and values to which Rammell refers are difficult to 'teach' as discrete content. Trying to teach such skills as 'communication' and such attributes as 'confidence' directly can often be counter-productive. Engagement with knowledge may have the indirect result of building communication and intellectual skills. The experience of intellectual struggle and success may lead to growth in one's confidence and abilities. But as Rammell rightly indicates, these are by-products of university life and not the prime aim. Whereas engagement with knowledge may have a transformative impact upon a student's understanding, narrowly defined core competencies are less likely to do so.

Little emphasis on sharing the knowledge and wisdom of society emerges from government HE policy. As well as technical skills, there is an emphasis upon higher education that 'is inclusive and progressive' (Thomas, 2001: 41). We are moving onto a different agenda here, concerned with the moral values associated with widening participation in HE to include a greater number in society. This can be seen explicitly in the demand for 'universities and colleges to continue to embody the values which are central to a democratic society' (DfES, 2003: 96). Inclusion, here, comes from the act of participation in education as opposed to any specifically academic or vocational outcomes that may be gained by the student. More recently, universities have been praised by the British government for 'passing on and preserving a set of shared societal values, including tolerance, freedom of expression and civic engagement. [Universities] have the capacity to provide intellectual leadership in our society, in areas such as the transition to a low carbon economy' (BIS, 2009: 18).

The focus of education is here shifted away from the preserving and passing on of a shared body of knowledge to the preserving and passing on of values. This can be seen in the recent inclusion of sustainable development as a cross-curricular theme in many taught modules or the emergence of courses such as 'Responsible Business'. This is a major shift in purpose and has repercussions in terms of academic and personal freedom. When values replace knowledge, education runs the risk of becoming reduced to indoctrination.

When participation in HE comes to be about personal transformation through acquiring skills and confidence, and instilling attitudes and values, more emphasis comes to be placed upon formal participation in university life, such as, registering attendance and actively participating in seminars and lectures. This is in the contrast to the approach of previous eras, when students may have considered their 'reading' for a degree as an act of albeit structured, almost private activity. The focus on active participation matches the agenda of the student-consumers, who campaign for value for money in terms of contact time with lecturers.

Yet back in the 1970s, Austrian philosopher Ivan Illich questioned the assumption that participation in terms of attendance and engagement with activities will automatically result in learning, an assumption which was first questioned in the 1970s. He challenged the notion that: 'the value of learning increases with the amount of input; and, finally, that this value can be measured and documented by grades and certificates' (Illich, 1970: 44). This assumption was further challenged by Swedish educator Torsten Husen who investigated the impact of raising the school leaving age, which was happening in many developed countries. Husen's research could establish no relationship between increased attendance and increased learning (Husen, 1974: 20–1). As a result of the focus upon attendance and participating in communal activity, building social capital between students becomes privileged above the act of creating individual cultural capital. Skills and values, such as communication and team work, become a substitute for engagement with subject knowledge.

This behaviourist focus upon attendance and activity can result in students being treated more like pupils in a school than students in a university, with registers, 'punishments' and group work emphasised over engagement with subject matter. Sandra describes her feelings when a lecturer marked her absent from a seminar as a 'punishment' for being late:

> It was the emphasis upon 'as a punishment'. I'm a forty-one-year-old mother of four. [...] Well there's me, I'm like busting a gut to make sure I do get here, juggling everything else and because I was late [...] I get punished.[19]

The emphasis here upon 'I'm a forty-one-year-old mother of four' shows this student's need to emphasise her adult status in relation to an exchange that left her feeling angry, patronised and infantilised. A focus upon attendance changes universities to little more than an extension of compulsory schooling.

Constructing students as participants in this way is not the same as perceiving students as learners. When students are seen as participants the emphasis of higher education is not upon the intellectual but the social, not upon learning but the act of engaging. Participation (no matter how active) does not necessarily equate to learning which can be a transformative process of intellectual and emotional struggle. Indeed, the emphasis upon participation may inadvertently promote the idea that physical presence alone is sufficient for learning to occur. Both participant and consumer status may both result in intellectual passivity on the part of students.

The satisfaction paradox

When the subject content of education is replaced by participation, intellectual engagement comes to be replaced by entertainment. The vacuum of intellectual struggle is filled by an expectation of consumer satisfaction. Alongside charters, a further source of information available to prospective students is data concerning the satisfaction of recent graduates with their institution. US universities have long published 'student satisfaction' data: Harvard University first collected and published student ratings of teaching in the mid–1920s, and this was followed by other institutions in the 1960s and 1970s as a 'student empowerment mechanism' (Singh, 2002: 68).

Since the early 1990s, there has been an international increase in monitoring student satisfaction (Dill, 2003: 2). In the UK the 1998 Higher Education Act saw the introduction of the National Student Survey (NSS) as a mechanism for measuring students' satisfaction with their programme of study, their lecturers, and the institution they attended. Measuring student satisfaction has here become a proxy for monitoring and regulating the student experience (Sabri, 2011). But in reality, it may not be the case that high levels of satisfaction are equated with a high *quality* student experience; the value of HE to individual students cannot be always be assessed until many years after graduation. 'Student satisfaction' in effect measures nothing more than how students subjectively feel at a particular point in time; their success on the programme to date (in terms of grades); and the extent to which any demands they have made of lecturers have been met. What such surveys do not provide is an objective measure of the quality of academic life.

UK government ministers have placed an increased focus on student satisfaction with the implementation of funding changes: 'As graduates are asked to contribute more than they do at present, the higher education sector should be more responsive to their choices and continuously improve the design and content of courses and the quality of their academic experience' (BIS, 2011: 14). The notion of being responsive to student choice reinforces the suggestion that lecturers exist to provide a satisfactory service to students rather than an experience that is intellectually challenging, complex and potentially transformative. It also means that students can dictate the academic content of subject disciplines. Elements of courses that are considered unpopular (or difficult) end up being phased out or moderated in favour of more popular (or less challenging) content.

As universities in the UK, and in the USA to a lesser extent, are ranked upon the basis of NSS results, producing league tables of satisfaction, universities often encourage students to make demands of lecturers so they can demonstrate having listened to the student voice and having modified the student experience accordingly. As well as the NSS, students are expected to complete course evaluation forms and are recruited onto staff/student liaison committees. Student representatives are inducted into their role by institutions and trained in how to behave by the NUS. The assumption is that this training empowers them to carry out their role more effectively, but it calls into question the representativeness of such students and assumes students and lecturers cannot talk through issues of concern without professional support. Such mechanisms demonstrate the extent to which universities have internalised the vision of students as customers more consistently than government ministers and seek to go further to solicit the opinions of students on the service they receive than is required by legislation.

As 'good' consumers, students are expected to take time to complete course evaluation forms and attend staff/student liaison committees to provide information on the satisfaction of the student experience and help institutions to improve the service for future customers. Universities respond to feedback from students and make changes to enhance their approval rating. It is noted as entirely positive by government ministers that: 'there is significant evidence of the impact of the NSS and institutions' own student feedback mechanisms in changing behaviour at institutional and departmental level' (BIS, 2009: 71). The assumption in this sentence is that using students to hold lecturers and institutions to account for the service they provide is a positive development. This could be interpreted as suggesting that students know better than lecturers what is needed in teaching and assessing particular courses.

This demand to produce satisfied consumers potentially has an impact upon pedagogy, as it may lead some lecturers to avoid making intellectual demands of their students and provide 'entertainment rather than education' (Morley, 2003: 90). As far back as 1852, the British theologian and writer Cardinal Newman indicated, in his seminal text *The Idea of a University*, the dangers of using the word 'educated' when in actual fact what is meant is 'amused, refreshed, soothed, put into good spirits and good humour, or kept from vicious excess' (Newman, 1959 [1852]: 164). The demand for satisfaction may be antithetical to education and the development of positive pedagogical relationships, as it implies that teaching should confirm what the student believes, rather than challenging students' assumptions in an intellectual process of transformation requiring sustained commitment.

The satisfaction of students is used in American universities to ascertain whether lecturers should be eligible for promotion or tenure. A lecturer's career and job security may depend upon him or her having satisfied students. This does not incentivise lecturers to confront students with intellectually challenging concepts or expose gaps in their knowledge. In the USA, the case of Professor Maranville, who was denied tenure by Utah Valley University after students complained that he asked them questions even when they had not indicated they wished to answer, and also that he made them work in teams, has attracted publicity (Basu, 2011). Lecturers seeking promotion and security are incentivised to make students satisfied through flattery and appeasement. This changes the nature of the relationship between students and lecturers (Trout, 1997; Naidoo and Jamieson, 2005) and may result in students losing a sense of responsibility for their own learning or opting out of academic risk-taking.

The focus on satisfaction can lead to intellectual passivity as lecturers are reluctant to make demands of students and students are not encouraged to jeopardise good grades by arguing for higher standards. As the American academic Michael Potts notes: 'If quality is sacrificed to customer satisfaction, with the attendant lack of quality teaching, tough grading, and student discipline, the college or university becomes merely a purveyor of expensive pieces of paper' (Potts, 2005: 63).

That institutions place attention so firmly upon the student experience reinforces the idea that the purpose of HE is the creation of satisfied consumers. This constructs the student consumer as someone who seeks immediate gratification in the act of being at university, rather than struggling with learning challenging content or the deferred intellectual gratification to be gained from having mastered a particular topic. Deferred gratification comes to be redefined solely as financial rather than intellectual reward. Intellectual work is perceived as a chore and the expectation is that the student consumer should be satisfied with the immediate student experience. 'Personal and intellectual fulfilment' (DfES, 2003: 14) is reduced to just one amongst many areas of potential satisfaction or dissatisfaction. This leaves universities 'competing to attract students on the basis of the excellent service they provide' (BIS, 2009: 17).

An irony here is that whilst the promotion of satisfaction may appear to be a *response* to students perceiving themselves as consumers, it also enhances trends towards the consumption model and constructs new generations of students as consumers. The more universities present themselves as responding to student demands, the more students are encouraged to see themselves as behaving correctly (doing what is expected) in demanding satisfaction (Furedi, 2009). Meanwhile, universities are placed in a contradictory position of having simultaneously to maintain both academic standards and customer satisfaction (Molesworth, Nixon and Scullion, 2009: 278).

Despite (or perhaps because of) such a focus upon student satisfaction, formal student complaints about universities to the Office of the Independent Adjudicator (OIA) are reported to have risen steeply in recent years (Shepherd and Williams, 2011). There is little evidence to suggest that the rise in student complaints is indicative of students having a poorer quality educational experience than those of previous generations. Instead there is evidence of a form of consumer activism: students have been led to believe that they are, as consumers, to expect a certain level of service and they are used to having their voices heard, and so are more prepared to complain if they feel they have been treated poorly. Students who complain are lauded as virtuous consumers, fully conversant with their rights (Furedi, 2009b: 1). Robert Behrens, Head of the OIA, attributes the sharp rise in complaints to students having a better understanding of their rights and 'knowing that what they have – a place on a degree course – is valuable and likely to cost more in the future' (Sugden, 2011). The expectation that complaints will rise as fees increase is made explicit with dire warnings to institutions that they 'must be better at dealing with complaints if they are to have any hope of students not feeling that they are being asked to pay more for less' (Sugden, 2011).

As universities increasingly set themselves up to respond to everything students say (the 'you said: we did' model of customer service), student complaints are always treated with the utmost seriousness. They are never just 'moans' or 'gripes' but serious indicators of institutional or departmental failure. One British university lecturer indicates: 'The NSS features highly in our publicity material, and the university is not at all keen to challenge the students' word; it matters more that they are happy than that they are appropriately educated'.[20] It is in the interests of universities to keep down the number of complaints, and American academic Paul Trout indicates they do this in part by making sure that academic standards are not high enough to cause students discomfort or endanger their academic 'success' (Trout, 1997: 50). This hints at the tension between the perceived academic purpose of the university and the university as a service purveying a commodity to customers. The fact that there can be such a thing as a breach of educational contract is 'based on the image of education as a service to be consumed, or as a commodity to be bought and sold, rather than an activity in which to participate' (Kaye, Bickel and Birtwistle, 2006: 87).

This is especially the case when a lecturer's career prospects (opportunities for tenure in the USA, promotion in the UK) are dependent upon positive student evaluations of their performance. If lecturers challenge students' outlook or make them feel uncomfortable by confronting them with new knowledge there is a danger that students will be dissatisfied and report this dissatisfaction in feedback forms and significantly in the UK, in the NSS, results of which comprise the basis of university league tables. However, a 'feel good factor' may not be 'conducive to intellectual growth' (Morley, 2003: 90). As Frank Furedi notes: 'one of the most distinct and significant dimensions of academic and intellectual activity is that it does not often give customers what they want' (Furedi, 2009: 2). Teaching according to the perceived desires of students 'negates even the possibility that higher education changes the individual's outlook' and becomes 'a mission of confirmation rather than transformation,' argue Molesworth, Nixon and Scullion (2009: 278). Michael Potts accuses college and university administrators of behaving unethically by replacing imparting knowledge with customer satisfaction (Potts, 2005: 63).

Those working within the academy must accept some responsibility for students perceiving of university in this way. It is up to lecturers to insist that learning is neither a simple matter of physical attendance nor likely to provide immediate satisfaction. By placing challenging subject matter, rather than students, at the heart of the university curriculum, lecturers can begin to reveal alternative models of what a university is for – not customer service or the delivery of a product, but far more satisfying and transformative a discovery and interpretation of all that is known about the world.

Endnotes

1 Interview with Joanna Williams.
2 Interview with Joanna Williams.
3 Valuing philosophy degrees: employability in higher education, (15/9/2011), Birmingham City University.

4 See http://humanities.exeter.ac.uk/english/undergraduate/employability/ [accessed 28/07/12]

5 See http://humanities.exeter.ac.uk/english/undergraduate/employability/ [accessed 28/07/12]

6 Ibid.

7 Interview with Joanna Williams.

8 Interview with Joanna Williams.

9 Interview with Joanna Williams.

10 Cited in *The Guardian* (26/09/06).

11 Interview with Joanna Williams.

12 Interview with Joanna Williams.

13 Interview with Joanna Williams.

14 Interview with Joanna Williams.

15 Interview with Joanna Williams.

16 Interview with Joanna Williams.

17 Interview with Joanna Williams.

18 Interview with Joanna Williams.

19 Interview with Joanna Williams.

20 Senior Lecturer British University, (17/3/11), in *Times Higher Education*.

5

A question of identity

This book has so far explored the construction of the student as consumer through the coming together of various social, political and economic trends. Throughout, I have largely assumed 'the student' as a single type with a homogenous identity. The past fifty years have witnessed unprecedented growth in the diversity of the student body and today there are more female, working-class, black and ethnic minority students in universities and other HE institutions than ever before. Labels such as 'traditional', 'non-traditional', 'new' and 'widening participation' are used, often euphemistically, to identify different groups of students. Students are also demarcated according to the institution they attend, with finely tuned distinctions drawn between students at Oxbridge, Russell Group and pre–1992 universities (former polytechnics) in the UK and between state, private, three- and four-year universities and community colleges in the US.

Different groups of students may be expected to react to fee-paying and consumer status in different ways. Whilst some students may welcome the consumer model of HE as enabling them to better fulfil their right to access a service, and empowering them to influence the nature of this service; for others the label 'consumer' is associated with the conspicuous excess of capitalism and therefore considered politically objectionable. However rejecting the label is not necessarily the same as rejecting consumer behaviour. For example, twenty-year-old Tom, whom we met in the previous chapter, sums up a common perception amongst students that to be labelled as a 'consumer' suggests that they have somehow 'bought' their degree and it is therefore 'worth less' than the degrees obtained by previous generations of students: 'I don't want to be rewarded for paying something because that's not going to get me anywhere.'[1] However, an irony apparent here is that at the same time as students may reject the label of consumer, they still value their degrees according to their worth in an instrumental sense of future career prospects, or future earnings potential, or – in Tom's words – 'where they will get you'. Thus it seems that some students appear to reject the label of 'consumer' in order to safeguard the exchange value of their degree in the post-graduation labour market and in so doing act as cannier consumers.

This chapter explores the question of student identity and what it means to be a student in the context of today's changed higher education sector. It begins with an historical examination of the shift in perceptions of 'the student'. Although the signifier 'student' has remained relatively constant, what is signified by this word has altered fairly radically in the past one hundred years. What it means to be a student at any given point in time is a social construction; it alters with the prevailing social and political conditions (Berger and Luckmann, 1966: 69) within society at that time. The financial, political and indeed psychological status of students is a creation of the social world; what it means to be a student today is different from previous historical eras and, even today, varies in different countries.

As Louise Morley notes: 'Whereas in the 1960s students were seen as change agents, radicals and transgressives, their identity at the beginning of the twenty-first century is described in the language of the market' (Morley, 2003: 83). Dennis Hayes also notes a change in how students are perceived: 'The changed conception of a student is not as an autonomous person embarking on the pursuit of knowledge, but as a vulnerable learner' (Hayes, 2009: 127). To consider students as consumers, customers, or even clients of the university, is distinct to the political and economic position of HE today.

From lonely scholars to service-users

The word 'student' originates from the Latin 'studium' meaning 'painstaking application'. The *Oxford English Dictionary* notes that in 1398 the word student was used to define someone engaged in or 'addicted to' studying.[2] Scholars living in secluded communities and devoting themselves to theological study may have engaged in such painstaking application to religious texts. The word was used from the end of the fifteenth century to indicate a person undergoing a course of study or instruction at a university. The word 'graduate' also came into use about this time to refer to someone with a university degree, and 'undergraduate' was consequently used for someone attempting to achieve this status. It should be noted that today, the word 'student' is used in America to refer to youngsters at school or college, and not exclusively to universities.

Prior to the mid-twentieth century, there appear to be two dominant images associated with students to emerge from historical sources, literature and contemporary news reports. The first is the dedicated scholar 'addicted' to his studies, or, later, the female equivalent, the 'bluestocking'. These students are portrayed as casting aside all material interests in a religious-like devotion to scholarship. The second is of young men from wealthy families far more interested in enjoying themselves than in intellectual pursuits. Such men were merely passing time in a hedonistic manner before having the status of gentleman conferred through graduation. In Jane Austen's *Pride and Prejudice*, this was the rogue Mr Wickham, who was supported through Cambridge University by his wealthy benefactor who wanted him to secure a 'gentleman's education' (Austen, 1813). The intention was for Wickham to take up a position within the Church, and a period at Cambridge was to be a useful precursor to this. Wickham himself demonstrates no interest whatsoever in religious study; for him, time spent at university was presumably a convenient way of postponing the demands of the real world and continuing to secure the financial support of his benefactor. The early twentieth century brought the dissolute image of Sebastian in Evelyn Waugh's *Brideshead Revisited*, who spends his time at Oxford engaged in anything other than studying.

Similar contrasting images of students emerge from America. Despite many students, especially those preparing for a career in the Church, demonstrating devoted application to their studies, a significant proportion 'often embraced a collegiate culture that had little to do with academic learning' (Arum and Roska, 2011). For these students their allegiance was to their peers through fraternities, clubs and social groups rather than to their discipline, the university faculty, or academic pursuits. The collegiality promoted through shared dormitories often became that of a social unit rather than a community of scholars. The popular perception is that for many students, years at university were spent engaging in hedonistic pursuits rather than academic endeavours. However, despite these polarised images of students, the reality for most was probably a mixture of revelling in the freedom to make new friends and experiment with living away from home or school, and time engaged in reading or studying to meet the demands of their lecturers.

As more public financial support became available to students from less wealthy backgrounds, the image of the upper-class hedonist, if he ever really existed, perhaps began to wane. University students in Britain were sometimes referred to as 'pupils' before the Second World War, a signifier more traditionally associated with children in schools (Truscott, 1945). This reminds us of the fact that universities had an *in loco parentis* responsibility to their students before the legal age of majority changed in the UK in 1969. However the use of the word *pupil* also carries an implication about the relationship of students to knowledge at this time. Pupils of the university are seen not so much as independent learners guided in their reading by lecturers, but as disciples of their teachers engaged in a rigorously determined programme of study. This is not to deny the application of such pupils to rigorous scholarship, but it is to note that lecturers were able to confidently assert a body of knowledge within their disciplinary area that they expected their students to master. The word 'student' could perhaps denote a more independent relationship to both lecturers and subject knowledge.

After the Second World War, the changes discussed in Chapter One to both the demographic characteristics of those who attended university, and the perceived purpose of higher education, began to challenge the image of students as either devoted to studies or rich youngsters addicted to their social life. A clear shift in the connotations of the word 'student' emerged in the 1960s in both the US and the UK. Students were presented in the media and public discourse in general as increasingly demanding, aggressive, assertive and self-confident. For the first time the word 'student' became correlated with more active, political nouns. The term 'student leader' first appeared in print sources in 1962 and 'student protest' in 1965. The terms 'student demonstrator', 'student revolution', 'student riot' and 'student violence' all first appeared in 1968.[3] 'Student activist' and 'student revolt' were both first used in print in 1969.

The image from this time is of students as radicals and change agents, making an impact upon the world in a social sphere that was greater than the confines of the university campus. However the impact of such political change reverberated around universities and led to the questioning not just of hierarchical institutional structures but crucially to the concept of knowledge itself. American academic Allan Bloom argues that such a political focus was detrimental to the pursuit of serious scholarship, as 'Commitment was understood to be profounder than science, passion than reason, history than nature, the young than the old' (Bloom, 1987: 34). Such a political change in the attitudes of students (and society more broadly) challenged not only the institutional hierarchies but also the core purpose of the university at the time. The idea of education as a conversation between the generations, the passing on of the collective knowledge of society to younger citizens, was challenged alongside the political and economic structures of society. An emotional commitment to a political principle was considered by many students to be more important a statement of their identity than the conclusions of dedicated and painstaking scholarship.

Since the 1980s, the challenge to a hierarchical concept of a body of knowledge handed from one generation to the next has continued to occur. There has been a rise in scepticism and relativism, perhaps as a reaction to 'the over-confident certainties of an earlier age' (Bailey, 2001: 162). The goals of traditional academic enquiry – rationality, objectivity, the pursuit of truth – have been undermined by postmodernists, social-constructivists and pragmatists (Bailey, 2001: 159).

On the other hand, taking part in political protest has become much less of a feature of student identity. There are many reasons for this shift in behaviour; most significant perhaps is that throughout society as a whole there is less appetite for politics, protests and demonstrations. Students are very much a part of society and cannot be expected to behave in a way that is out of sync with the prevailing social mood. Yet perhaps due to the legacy of the 1960s, there is an expectation that students *should* be involved in protests and thus a perceived need to offer explanations for their lack of political engagement. Former British NUS President Aaron Porter explains students' lack of involvement in political protest as resulting from the experience of being a student today: 'The pressures on a twenty-first century student in terms of study and part-time work means the romanticism of the 1960s protestor is a world away' (Sugden and Rennison, 2011). The logic of this argument is that students are politically motivated but simply lack the time and money necessary to engage in protests: 'students now can't afford lengthy protests. Unlike students in the 60s, most of them have part-time jobs to go to,' suggests one British commentator (Redmond, 2009).

Such a view serves to portray the experience of university students in the 1960s as a 'golden age' in contrast to the harsh financial realities experienced by today's students: 'the parents of the current generation of undergraduates could use their university years – assuming they had them – for experimentation, for politicisation, for a sense of collective purpose' (Wignall, 2006). Yet it is worth questioning whether students in the 1960s and 1970s really engaged in collective political protest simply because they had the time and money to do so – and conversely whether students today do not engage in politics simply because they are too busy studying or working for money. Although many students in the UK were lucky enough to benefit from generous financial state support in the 1960s and 1970s, they did not pay for the en-suite accommodation, the mobile phone contracts, computer equipment or supermarket deliveries that many of today's students enjoy. Many of today's students do still receive state financial support, albeit in the form of income-contingent repayable loans.

It rather seems that the expectation of how much money is needed to sustain a student lifestyle has changed alongside less romanticised views of collective living and a greater individualisation of the student experience. Up until the mid–1990s it was common for first-year undergraduates in halls of residence to share bedrooms as well as bathrooms. Yet there is an assumption that today's students are too preoccupied with worrying about future debt repayment, or too focused upon securing a degree that will make them employable, or too burdened with immediate financial problems, to afford the luxury of time spent protesting. By this argument, increasing tuition fees will make student protests in the future *less*, not more, likely.

In reality, for previous generations and for students in other countries today, full-time employment or extreme financial hardship does not prevent people from protesting over issues about which they feel passionately. It may well be the case that in an increasingly a-political culture, students have little motivation to engage in ideological battles. Bloom commented that in the 1960s commitment was thought to be profounder than science. In the twenty-first century, commitment is perhaps viewed by many students with as much suspicion as science. In 2009, then President of the University of Liverpool's Guild of Students, Danielle Grufferty suggested a reason for a lack of student protest:

Two million marched in February 2003 calling for no war in Iraq, and what became of it? [...] When students campaigned to keep the cap on university tuition fees, we drew out huge numbers. Nevertheless, the vote was lost. People keep targeting students for their apathy, but when nothing we say or do seems to affect government policy, what is our alternative? (Redmond, 2009)

The model of the anxiety-fuelled, debt-burdened student-consumer may simply provide radical commentators with a more palatable explanation for a lack of protest than a broader disillusionment with politics.

This is not to suggest that students are completely apathetic today. Instead of the mass demonstrations of past decades, the form of protest today is often on a different scale, such as the occupation of university buildings by small groups of students, or more passive displays of support such as signing up to the Facebook pages of chosen causes. There has also been a shift in the purpose and motivation of such public demonstrations that do take place. Whereas in the 1960s students campaigned for civil rights or against war and nuclear weapons, in recent years the biggest student protests have been over the increase in tuition fees in the UK or campaigning for student loan debt forgiveness in the US. It may be the case that consumer status works to restrict the sphere of influence for students seeking to be politically engaged.

The perception that students are consumers may serve to impose limits, if not upon the topics students want to protest about, then certainly to the media interest in such protests. Whilst consumer-status legitimates complaints about the student experience it inadvertently calls into question the assumption that students will have their voices heard on a range of other issues. This has led Louise Morley to suggest there has been a 'domestication of the student voice' (Morley, 2003: 90). Certainly today's active campaigning students, who are heralded as agents of change within their institutions, are quick to learn the bureaucratic language of agenda items, assessment patterns, learning outcomes and programme monitoring, and are more likely to be found sitting on staff student liaison committees than on picket lines. This domestication of the student voice and limiting of campaigning confirms the consumer identity of students rather than challenging it.

Changing values

Students campaigning against tuition fees or student debt risk being portrayed in the media as self-interested and only arguing for the maintenance of their own privileged position. They are considered to be selfless and worthy of public praise, however, when campaigning for free access to higher education to be extended to more of the population as a 'right'. The idea that all people should have a right to higher education has become a popular cause in recent decades. But it is problematic to consider education as a right because it is not a tangible commodity that can be given to people. If education is defined as the product of the relationship between student and lecturer, or engagement in intellectual processes, it becomes far more difficult to determine what exactly one has a 'right' to expect. The demand for a right to higher education, as opposed to schooling, could also raise questions of access. It may be the case that a right cannot exist as such unless it can be applied universally to all of the population. Yet higher education is by nature discriminatory on the basis of academic ability, or at very least, potential academic ability. Applicants are expected to demonstrate the intellectual potential to be able to cope with the demands of university study prior to admission into a university.

Arguably, at a time of increased tuition fees and reduced graduate employment prospects, the exercising of academic discrimination by university admissions officers becomes a more important responsibility, to prevent individuals who are unsuited to a degree course from expenditure of their time and personal resources. In many ways learning at university occurs as a result of individual application. Yet these principles are brushed aside in the assumption that higher education is a 'right'. If rights are tangible outcomes – 'an object or a thing to be possessed' (Kaye, Bickel and Birtwistle, 2006: 97) – then there is a danger that students no longer expect to take responsibility for their own education, but can demand that lecturers ensure that they learn. In arguing for the fulfilment of rights, higher education again becomes reduced to a matter of contact hours with lecturers and the timescale within which assessed work is returned, for example. The more education is considered something that can be 'given' or 'done' to someone, the more it is conceived of as a commodity with students constructed as consumers, waiting to receive the outcome of education rather than to engage in its processes. If students perceive of a place at university as the fulfilment of their rights, then a degree becomes seen as their entitlement irrespective of application, effort or intellectual ability.

The notion of a university degree as an entitlement is further reinforced by some apparent critics of the employability agenda who argue that the purpose of the HE sector is to bring about social justice. If the possession of a degree is considered necessary for participation in the labour market, then, it is argued, being denied access to a degree certificate, prevents people from earning the money required to participate in society and reinforces social and class divisions. However, this view of HE separates a degree certificate (a tangible product) from intellectual engagement; the degree certificate becomes an individual entitlement as a prerequisite for social justice and a fair society, rather than recognition of an individual's ability to participate in building disciplinary knowledge.

Ironically, at the same time as HE itself comes to be seen as a *product* – and a product to which all are entitled – there has been an increase in campaigns against the more obvious encroachment of business interests into academia. It seems that the more a degree certificate becomes a commodity, the less many within the HE sector wish to be associated with other forms of commercialisation. In 1996, there were protests in the UK in response to Cambridge University accepting money from British-American Tobacco to fund a Professorship in International Relations. More recently in the UK the philosopher A. C. Grayling's establishment of the private HE college, The New College of Humanities, for which he intends to charge students double the fee-cap imposed upon 'public' institutions, has provoked outcry amongst sections of the liberal media (Eagleton, 2011). Such political distaste represents a view that private money is 'bad' and public money is 'good', despite the fact that government money may come with far more political strings attached. In recent years funding bodies that distribute government money to academics in the form of grants for particular research projects have asserted criteria that are much more explicitly in keeping with the political agenda of government. Yet there persists an uncritical belief held by many academics that money from the state is 'good' and independent or private finance is 'bad', as it must be tainted by the interests of capitalist business.

Campaigns against tuition fees, and for student debt forgiveness, have coincided with a growing popularity for anti-capitalist protests in general. In the USA there have been some student protests against excessive commercialisation on campus, leading American academic Astin to note: 'the emergence of a small but rapidly growing minority of students who are concerned about a variety of social issues and who are inclined to become actively involved in working with these issues' (Astin, 1991: 141). An American campaign group, Students Against University Commercialism and Exploitation (SAUCE) campaigned in 2000 against Rutgers University having entered into a $10 million marketing contract with Coca-Cola. Members of SAUCE held a demonstration over the contract and gave away alternative drinks, including Pepsi. They argued that the university had 'sold out': 'The university should exist for students and faculty, not for a corporation,' argued one member of SAUCE, continuing, 'We weren't trying to take over the president's office – we just wanted to offer students a choice of what kind of soda they drink' (Hardi, 2000).

Such protests tend to present capitalism as a problem of individual consumption with the solution being seen to lie in individuals making better informed consumer choices. In this anti-capitalist discourse higher education, as a purchasable commodity, becomes reduced to 'just one round of consumer desire in an endless series of consumption experiences' (Molesworth, Nixon and Scullion, 2009: 280). Discussion as to the nature and purpose of higher education become focused on the charging of tuition fees, or even more specifically the level at which fees are set, or the rate of interest accrual on student debt. Yet, as this book has explored, the charging of tuition fees is only one small part of the transformation of students into consumers.

Despite the occasional surfacing of such protests, for the most part today's students are portrayed as increasingly self-interested and focused upon their future careers and earnings potential at the expense of concern with either broader political issues or dedication to scholarship within their chosen disciplines. An annual survey of the attitudes of American under-graduate students shows that the proportion seeking a college education in order to be 'very well off financially' increased from 37 per cent of students in the early 1970s to 78 per cent in 2009. Whilst it is undoubtedly the case that some students have always sought higher education as a means of securing upward social mobility or in order to enter a particular profession, there are two notable changes here. The first is quantitative: an almost doubling in the proportion of students who seek financial remuneration as a result of their studies. The second change is more qualitative. In seeking to be financially wealthy, students are not expressing any inherent interest in a particular career, such as wanting to be a doctor or a lawyer or a journalist, because they think these might be worthwhile careers in themselves. Rather, the only worthwhile goal is seen to be the accruing of a high salary.

In a similar vein, the reason for attending university which has shown the largest decline among American university students over the same period is 'developing a meaningful philosophy of life'. This has fallen from 73 per cent of students who claimed this as a reason for entering university in the early 1970s to 48 per cent in 2009. 1989 was the year that the goal of attending college in order to 'gain a general education and appreciation of ideas' reached its lowest point in the history of the survey (Astin, 1991: 132). It would perhaps be all too easy to blame students themselves for these changes in attitudes and bemoan the fact that young people nowadays are too individualistic, materialistic and self-centred and have been lured by propaganda of the market into seeking satisfaction in purely monetary reward. However, we must remind ourselves that as discussed in Chapter 3, the message students are given from schools, the media and government policy is that the main purpose of higher education is to secure increased earnings potential and job security. It should come as little surprise, then, that students buy into this discourse, especially as such ideas are rarely challenged upon arrival at university. However, such survey results also reflect changes beyond the world of higher education; they hint at a general decline in political idealism. There is no longer a strongly held belief amongst young people that they can make a positive impact upon the world; often it is assumed as arrogant to even consider trying.

Another popular image of students today is that while they may not be as hedonistic as previous generations, they are certainly not spending a great deal of time on their studies. Rather, students are presented as spending time socialising, engaging in social networking through the internet, or earning money through employment in coffee shops or bars. Empirical evidence supports suggestions that academic effort on the part of under-graduate students has dramatically declined in recent decades. In the early 1960s students in the US spent roughly forty hours per week on academic pursuits. Today this figure is just twenty-seven hours per week. In 1961, 67 per cent of students studied for more than twenty hours a week. By 1981 this figure had reached 44 per cent and in 2010 only one in five (20 per cent) spent more than 20 hours a week studying (Arum and Roska, 2011). Similarly in the UK, in 2007 a survey reported that students spent on average twenty-six hours per week on all academic work including attending lectures and seminars, reading, researching and completing assessment tasks (Doughty, 2007). This average figure hides huge variations between the demands of different courses and institutions.

Rather than challenging the lack of time students spend on academic work and thus running the risk that students will note dissatisfaction with their chosen modules, lecturers tend to accommodate to these reduced notions of how much time students can be expected to put into their studies independently. Lecturers will, for example, often recommend students read chapters of books which are made available to download, rather than whole texts which are only available from the library. Similarly lecture notes are often made available to students, undermining any assumption they will be able to take their own notes.

The anti-elitist university

As discussed in the previous chapter, lecturers sometimes appear reluctant to criticise undergraduates for poor academic performance or lack of application for fear of being penalised by students in satisfaction surveys or teaching evaluation questionnaires. More publicly there is perhaps a fear that criticising students may pave the way for accusations of elitism and seeking a return to the days before widening participation policies and the arrival of 'non-traditional' students on campus. There is an assumption that, as society no longer has an elite HE sector, lecturers can no longer have the same expectations of what all students will be capable of achieving, and that to teach and assess non-traditional students using traditional educational methods will put them at an inherent disadvantage with their peers.

This is wrong for two reasons. Firstly it assumes that 'traditional' students are still capable of challenging work and are aware of the commitment to academic pursuits that is required. Instead, the evidence presented above suggests that a drop in the amount of time studying is not just reflective of a move to a mass HE system with different types of students – all types of students recorded less study time than in previous decades.

Secondly, such an assumption suggests that non-traditional students (that is, working-class, black or ethnic minority students or students with disabilities) are less capable of being able to reach the same academic standards as traditional students, and that therefore the expectations of all students must be lowered to avoid damaging the self-esteem of non-traditional students. Yet there is no evidence to suggest that non-traditional students should be academically less capable than those with a family history of university attendance stretching back through the generations. Whilst some non-traditional students may lack the cultural capital of their more middle-class or expensively schooled peers and initially find it challenging to negotiate a new environment and new expectations, there is no reason to assume that non-traditional students are ultimately capable of achieving less and need the quantity or difficulty of educational content to be reduced for their convenience.

The reluctance to expose presumed intellectual weaknesses of non-traditional students in part motivates the breaking down of assessment methods and course requirements into very specific terms. There is an assumption that a lack of transparency around assessment methods places non-traditional students at a disadvantage to their 'traditional' classmates, who may have prior knowledge as to how to negotiate essay titles, for example. Such tacit knowledge, it is argued, needs to be made explicit for their less fortunate peers (and therefore for all students). However, such making explicit of expected intellectual outcomes reinforces the instrumentalism described in the previous chapter. Lecturers with an anti-elitist bent meet students who seek a degree product, or a certificate of credentials to trade in a post-graduation labour market, rather than any intellectual desire to pursue knowledge for its own sake and the result is collective consent to the lowering of academic expectations.

For many students, this reinforces their aim to secure the highest degree classification in a way that requires the least intellectual effort. Their energy and focus is instead reserved for negotiating their way through undergraduate programmes, selecting the topics, assessment methods, and lecturers most likely to enable them to achieve high marks. The intellectual endeavour becomes one of 'controlling college', rather than study within a particular discipline (Astin, 1991: 130). For students who consider their focus to be negotiating their way through university, HE comes to be about the fulfilment of their rights in a technical sense, such as a 'right' to a specified number of contact hours with lecturers or a 'right' to have assessed work returned within a specified period of time. Energy that may in the past have been used for independent study becomes consumed with ensuring that these so-called rights are fulfilled.

Such a shift in the focus of students' aims in attending university is both reflected in and encouraged by a change in the language government ministers use to refer to students. As discussed in Chapter Two, UK government policy documents have in recent years referred to students as 'clients' of a university. The word 'client' has two meanings: a person or organisation using the services of a professional person or company, and a person dealt with by social or medical services.[4] Both meanings are problematic when applied to students. The first suggests that lecturers are service providers like architects or accountants, and that students are merely the passive recipients of a pre-prepared learning experience. Although the first definition of 'client' is most likely the one intended in policy documents, it is also worth noting the extent to which higher education is increasingly fashioning a therapeutic relationship with students, who are perceived as vulnerable to a number of financial, social and existential pressures (Ecclestone and Hayes, 2009). Such a changed relationship with students is also apparent in the use of the word 'learner' to refer to students.

Individuals attending university are today frequently referred to as learners, rather than students. This is perhaps intended to denote a form of equality; everyone in the institution can be described as a learner in one form or another as the word is sufficiently vague as to encompass the knowledge people gain from all the experiences they have in their daily lives. The concept of learning therefore denotes little that is discipline, subject or even educationally specific. The term 'learner' also, then, denotes a change in the way students are seen in relation to knowledge. Instead of looking outwards and discovering things about the world, learners can look inwards and learn about themselves. Instead of being the disciples of their lecturers, like university 'pupils' before the Second World War, today's learners are more focused upon their own 'learning journey'. This can be encouraged by lecturers who argue the goal of higher education is personal transformation in the absence of a rigorous relationship to subject knowledge, and universities that argue that league tables should measure the 'value added' by the institution from the point at which students started their degree programme. This may serve to diminish the standing of knowledge within the academy, as objective measures of what students know or do not know are replaced by more subjective measures of what knowledge means to individuals and how much more they know in relation to their own previous performance.

HE policymakers assume that learners have an understanding of the workings of the HE sector sufficient to enable them to make informed choices regarding the selection of institution to attend and degree programme to complete in order to secure their chosen future course of employment. There is clearly a belief behind the drive for universities to publish ever more detailed data on the content and teaching of courses offered that all students lack is information to enable them to make rational decisions about their educational futures. Similarly, there is an assumption from institutions that students possess both the subject knowledge and pedagogical understanding to effectively select their own degree programmes through piecing together an array of different optional modules and also to make informed evaluations of their lecturers' performance. Both of these assumptions are groundless.

The idea that student choice will drive up the quality of the HE sector in the UK implies that students are capable of recognising quality within higher education and that they will give feedback and make educational (and financial) decisions according to this understanding of quality. In the British government's 2011 higher education policy document, *Students at the Heart of the System*, it is argued that putting 'financial power into the hands of learners makes student choice meaningful' (BIS, 2011: 5) and that 'Our reforms are designed to deliver a more responsive higher education sector in which funding follows the decisions of learners' (BIS, 2011: 8). The assumption is that students will make rational economic decisions as educational consumers within a university marketplace. The image of such a student is criticised by British academics Carole Leathwood and Paul O'Connell for being constructed as male, middle class and able-bodied, 'an autonomous individual unencumbered by domestic responsibilities, poverty or self-doubt [. . .] rooted in white western cultural constructions of an independent self [. . .] the new subject of free-market neo-liberalism, fully responsible for his/her own 'choices' and future' (Leathwood and O'Connell, 2003: 599).

However, if we read recent policy documents closely, it becomes apparent that a far more contradictory view of students emerges. On the one hand, learners are presented as rational actors within an educational free market. But within the same documents, learners are also presented as vulnerable in the face of the market and in need of national government to act as an arbitrator in the face of universities that may seek to exploit potential consumers. The introduction of student charters and the publication of Key Information Set data, for example, have been proposed by government ministers as a mechanism for protecting the interests of students and ensuring they get value for money from the institution they attend. In the 2011 policy document the image of the rational economic learner is juxtaposed with 'non-traditional higher education learners including mature and part-time students' (BIS, 2011: 46) and recognition of the need to offer 'support for adult learners' (BIS, 2011: 61). Indeed, the signifier 'learner', when introduced seemingly in preference to the term 'student' by the previous Labour government, was most frequently correlated with the word 'support', in phrases such as: 'supporting progression for disadvantaged gifted learners' (BIS, 2009: 33); 'to strengthen the support that universities provide for those learners' (BIS, 2009: 33); and 'students must be supported to become independent learners' (BIS, 2009: 73). The word 'support' appears 154 times in the 115 pages of the Labour Government's 2009 *Higher Ambitions* document. This calls into question the assumption that policymakers consider learners to be economically rational, autonomous beings.

Perhaps one reason for the debate as to whether students are unfairly presented as overly rational stems from a changed meaning of rationality in relation to higher education. In the introduction to the 2011 White Paper it is claimed:

The English higher education tradition has particularly stressed the autonomy and independence of both learners and institutions, more than some other national traditions. In this Chapter, we look at how higher education institutions can create a learning community where engagement of students is encouraged, their feedback valued and complaints resolved transparently and as soon as possible. (BIS, 2011: 33)

Here we see how the use of the word 'autonomy' is first used to describe learners and institutions imbued with the spirit of academic freedom and intellectual risk-taking, capable of following rational debate and presenting logical arguments. In the second sentence autonomy comes to be re-presented as a matter of students having their feedback heard and their complaints resolved and independence as engaging with a learning community. As Morley asks: 'While students might gain more consumer leverage in terms of turnaround time for essays etc., are they in danger of losing more complex identities as scholars and social agents?' (Morley, 2003: 92).

Critics of recent policy documents who decry the 'white, western, able-bodied, masculine' presentation of students are perhaps at risk of confusing intellectual autonomy (or the potential to exercise academic autonomy) with the ability of students to make rational pedagogic choices. Leathwood and O'Connell criticise the concept of the 'independent learner' as excluding non-traditional students (Leathwood and O'Connell, 2003: 610) but perhaps more excluding is the notion that non-traditional students are any less capable of aiming for intellectual autonomy and exercising rationality in relation to academic debate than their more financially privileged peers.

It is the exercising of individual autonomy that means the construction of students as consumers is far from inevitable. If students were simply a product of their circumstances then their identity would indeed be both fixed and homogenous. Instead, individual agency means that despite much government policy assuming students welcome consumer status as enabling them to make increased demands of the institutions they attend; in reality not all students wish to be labelled as consumers of HE. The vocabulary of the 'student experience', 'student charters' and 'employability' may all help to create the impression that HE is a product to be consumed and may lead to the adoption by some students of a consumerist attitude, vocabulary or behaviour and the internalisation of such beliefs about their status within institutions. Yet student identity is not fixed but is open to question and to challenge. Students are able to exercise individual autonomy, to resist dominant discourses and to forge their own identity. To simply see all students as consumers would be to deny the role of individual autonomy in the creation of student identity. Student identity is formed through a relationship between individual autonomy and prevailing social conditions:

students may choose whether or not to act as consumers, although they make this choice in circumstances which are determined by the institutions they attend and the broader social and cultural context.

Acknowledging the autonomy of students and their ability to determine whether or not to position themselves as consumers is important because students are all too often viewed by government ministers and academics as a pre-determined product of the labels attached to them – for example, 'non-traditional'– and the expectations held of students are adjusted accordingly. Recent research indicates that many students reject not just the label of consumer but also the associated behaviour, and value that which is personally transformative about their HE experience (Ashwin, Abbas and McLean, 2011). Interestingly, the desire for learning to be personally transformative was found amongst students at all types of universities. That is, it is not just middle-class students at top-ranking universities who can financially afford the 'luxury' of an education which is personally trans-formative, but working-class students at lower-ranking institutions desire this too. It is not the case that all non-traditional students are just interested in HE for job prospects or earning potential.

One problem with this is that in the absence of rigorous engagement with subject knowledge, goals of personal transformation become reduced to a focus upon the self alone. This paves the way for education to become preoccupied with the psychological and individual autonomy is further eroded through a 'therapeutic turn' (Ecclestone and Hayes, 2009) that assumes vulnerability in students. This takes many forms and can be seen in new initiatives such as transition management when students first arrive at university or are about to leave, offers of counselling when sensitive issues are covered as part of taught content, and a pedagogic concern with the self-esteem of students. The therapeutic turn is also reflected in dimin-ished expectations of what students are intellectually capable of achieving. Rather than reading lists indicating whole books students must purchase or obtain from the library, students are guided towards particular chapters which they are often then able to download from the institution's intranet. As already noted, assessment tasks are often structured around the need for students to meet specific learning outcomes, encouraging students to adopt an instrumental approach to their academic work which does not stray beyond the knowledge which is predetermined at the start of the particular module. Yet despite a reduction in the intellectual demands made of students, and of the amount of time individual students engage in academic pursuits, there has been no reduction in the number of students achieving high level degree passes. Indeed, in the UK, degree pass marks have in fact gone up over the past decade. In America likewise the reported decline in study hours bears no relation to a decline in pass marks or GPAs; on the contrary, these have continued to rise.

Ironically, rather than reduced expectations upon students boosting their sense of their own academic abilities and intellectual esteem, many students internalise such low expectations of what they may be capable of achieving. Senior tutors at the University of Kent report a rise in the number of students seeking extensions to coursework assignments on the grounds of stress, anxiety or depression. Such states become normalised for young people and their declaration incentivised through allowances given by tutors. This is not to deny the reality of students' anxieties about accumulating debt prior to entering an uncertain labour market. However, in previous social eras such anxiety may have resulted in the political radicalisation of the student body or an individual determination to hold down employment as well as securing good grades; it would not have been automatically medicalised through diagnoses of metal health problems. Lecturers in Adult Education are familiar with the stereotype of the mature student who works long hours in employment yet will still be the best-prepared and the first to arrive for class. It is not the anxiety suffered by some students alone that suggests a diminished sense of self but the form the anxiety takes.

One explanation given for the increase in stress and anxiety experienced by students is the necessity for students to negotiate their way through a higher education marketplace. The onus upon students to think and act as consumers at all times can be experienced by some as an added pressure. Sociologist Zygmunt Bauman describes portrayals of consumers as veering between the extremes of 'cultural dupes or dopes' and 'heroes of modernity', and the same applies to students as consumers. At the first extreme, consumers are represented as anything but autonomous individuals: they are shown instead to be hoodwinked by fraudulent promises, enticed, seduced, pushed and otherwise manoeuvred by blatant or surreptitious, but invariably extraneous, pressures. At the other extreme, the student-consumer encapsulates all the virtues for which modernity wishes to be praised – like rationality, robust autonomy, capacity for self-definition and rugged self-assertion (Bauman, 2008: 11–12).

Conclusions

The concept of student identity in the twenty-first century is clearly complex. It is underpinned by intertwined changes in the meaning of higher education and the imposition of market values which seek to transform students into consumers. Bauman comments that 'consumers are cut away from and placed outside the universe of their prospective objects of consumption' (Bauman, 2008: 12). This applies to education: the identity of consumer serves only to distance students from subject knowledge. Furthermore, the relationship of students to both knowledge and consumption belies a broader debate, which is the sense of the student as a rational, autonomous subject. In challenging the model of the student as consumer, it is easy to knock down the image of the rational decision maker; but when this comes at the expense of being able to defend the notion of the independent learner academically free to pursue independent intellectual thought and logical academic arguments, we undermine the very core of higher education.

Endnotes

1 Interview with Joanna Williams.

2 Second edition, 1989; online version September 2011. <http://www.oed.com. chain.kent.ac.uk/view/Entry/192056> [accessed 05 December 2011]. Earlier version first published in *New English Dictionary*, 1919.

3 Second edition, 1989; online version September 2011. <http://www.oed.com. chain.kent.ac.uk/view/Entry/192056> [accessed 05 December 2011].

4 Oxford Dictionary of English.

6

Customer care

Traditionally, most students have entered university in the years immediately after leaving school. In the academic year 2009/10, 41.5 per cent of first year UK students were aged just eighteen or younger.[1] Because of this universities have, since as far back as the fourteenth century, played a role in managing the transition of youngsters to adulthood. This has variously taken an academic, moral, social, cultural or disciplinary focus, depending upon the historical era and the perceived purpose of higher education at the time (Silver, 2004: 124).

This chapter explores the impact consumer status has upon students' transition to adulthood and the institutional management of this process. It could be argued that treating students as fee-paying customers accelerates emerging adult autonomy, as youngsters have a financial power that commands they be taken seriously. However, I argue that often consumer status often comes to be experienced as infantilising by students. High levels of tuition fees and living expenses may mean that some students experience a prolonged period of financial dependency upon parents and this may lead parents to assume they are co-consumers in their child's education. Some universities may respond to parents' (and sometimes students') demands for customer care by resuming a position of *in loco parentis* over students, whereby the institution assumes parental responsibility for students' welfare. Furthermore, the notion that students are 'at the heart' of higher education may confirm the egotistical assumptions of the adolescent rather than challenging such attitudes and encouraging students to realise the historical context of their place in the world in relation to other people.

Parents as co-consumers

So far in this book I have discussed the concept of the *student* as consumer, yet institutions, policy documents and the media frequently make reference to groups other than students as the consumers of higher education. The website of the University of the Arts in Philadelphia is typical in that it expresses the institution's commitment 'to providing consumers (students, parents, counsellors, researchers, legislators and the general public) with easy-to-access information that can be used in making informed decisions about higher education'.[2] The most frequently cited consumers alongside students are parents. Almost every British and American university website now has a section specifically aimed at parents. Universities may put just as much time and money into marketing themselves to parents as to potential students. Indeed, for some, parents are considered the main customers of a university, as indicated by an article published in the *Welsh Journal of Education* in 2002 entitled *Keeping the 'Customer' Satisfied: Parents in the higher education marketplace* (Pugsley and Coffey, 2002). However ironically this title may be intended, it hints at a broader truth: it is parents who are the presumed recipients of a university's 'service'.

The positioning of parents as consumers, or at very least as co-consumers, alongside their children is evident in government policy. The word 'parents' appears some fourteen times in the British government's 2011 policy document *Students at the Heart of the System* in reference to parents being provided with information or having their expectations met. In this way, parents are presented as consumers. Statements such as 'we believe it is reasonable for students and their parents to expect higher education institutions to make student welfare a priority' (BIS, 2011: 35) suggest that parents are recipients of a university's service. In addition, this statement hints at the changed emphasis that is created by the involvement of parents: student *welfare* becomes a focus alongside academic and vocational pursuits.

The equivalent publication from 2003, *The Future of Higher Education*, does make reference to parents but this is mainly either to students who are parents themselves, or to the proposed changes in funding arrangements, which would mean that parents did not have to make an up-front financial contribution to the cost of their child's education. In the space of just eight years, then, parents have gone from being reassured that financially they are *not* needed to play such a role in the lives of their student offspring to being placed centre-stage alongside their children as consumers of a university service.

In making the shift in the perception of the role of parents, the British government has perhaps again been influenced by the American Department for Education's 2006 document, *A Test of Leadership* ('The Spellings Report'). In this document, frequent references are made to parents who are very much presented as consumers of higher education, often appearing before students in statements such as: 'Despite increased attention to student learning results by colleges and universities and accreditation agencies, parents and students have no solid evidence, comparable across institutions, of how much students learn in colleges' (Spellings, 2006: 30). It is parents, before students, who are presented as requiring evidence of results.

Such a changed positioning of parents to co-consumers of a university experience is widely reported in the media of both countries: 'Parents, particularly those from middle-class backgrounds, are behaving more and more like consumers: they pay the money, they expect to see results', reports one newspaper (Smith-Squire, 2008). It is interesting to note that the product described here is not attendance at a particular university or a certain type of experience; rather, it is simply 'results'. The description of what parents are presumed to be seeking in relation to the payment of fees, as with students, hinges around value for money and particularly on future employment prospects. Parents are assumed to want a return upon their investment in university costs and for their child to secure future employment in return for the financial outlay.

This inclusion of parents in the consumer role appears, at least in part, as a natural consequence of demands for ever higher levels of tuition fees, which will, for some students, be met by their parents' bank accounts. Parents paying large sums of money towards the cost of their child's education may feel as if they have a financial stake in their child's university experience and then feel entitled to have a degree of influence over where, what and how their child studies. The pressure group College Parents of America asks: 'as the cost of education continues to rise, is it reasonable to expect that "students" alone will remain the premier recipients of service, and to receive the respect accorded with such status?' There is much that is interesting in this question, not least the assumption that students receive a service and that consumer status accords respect. It can only be presumed that the quotation marks around the word 'students' are not intended ironically. The answer provided to the question 'is it reasonable' is:

> [...] probably not. The parent, who is footing a substantial amount of the college bill, is gaining ground, at least in small part due to our efforts at College Parents of America. But if parents are to attain fuller recognition of their 'education consumer' status, shouldn't they be better informed so that they can knowledgeably weigh in on such basic questions as increased grant aid, or bigger-picture issues such as how a school can adopt the ever-elusive 21st-century business model?[3]

Here we can see how the demand to be better informed appears as a logical response to 'footing the bill'.

In the UK there are similar demands for increased status for parents as consumers linked to the payment of tuition fees, as this editorial from *Times Higher Education* demonstrates:

> But £27,000 is a lot of money, which is why most 18-year-olds will not be allowed to spend it alone. Parents will be the true consumers of higher education. Expect concerns about employability to become shriller. What parents would want to entrust their still-maturing offspring with

such spending power and then find that they return home after three years to take up full-time residence on the sofa? Parents will do their utmost to ensure that this investment results in gainful employment.[4]

A particular view of students, and their relationship with their parents, seems to emerge from such quotations. Students are presented as immature, financially irresponsible and uncertain what is in their own best interests. Such students are presented as in dire need of knowledgeable parents, who can 'weigh in' with demands that universities make their offspring employable.

The age at which many students typically leave compulsory school and enter university coincides with the age when young adults seek to establish their emotional, financial and practical independence. They may be expected to challenge the perception that they are immature and perhaps also to challenge parental authority as they seek to make their own decisions about their life-course. The positioning of parents as co-consumers can make it harder for young people to do this. Melissa, 19-year-old undergraduate, relates a conversation with her father in relation to course choice:

> My dad wasn't so sure about Psychology because he thought it wasn't necessarily something that could lead into a lot of money. He said 'You're going to spend three years and a lot of money, are you going to be able to find something afterwards?'[5]

The interesting thing here is not so much that Melissa acted upon her father's advice – she followed her own instincts and studied Psychology – but more that the words of her father linger sufficiently to emerge unprompted. The questioning of Melissa's future employment prospects and the need to see her degree in terms of future employability is still shaped by the concerns of her father and probably reinforced by lecturers and an institutional focus upon employability which meets the concerns of her father.

From the students' perspective, having parents make a financial contribution towards tuition fees or living expenses may, for some, enhance a sense of dependency that youngsters trying to establish their independence may not welcome. This comment from Sarah, a first-year biochemist, is typical of many:

> I mean even my accommodation, the maintenance loan didn't even cover my accommodation, so my parents are making up that shortfall and then giving me an allowance.[6]

Despite having taken out all available loans, many students are left in a position of financial dependency which can be experienced as infantilising: the phrase 'giving me an allowance' places the 'me' as passive object in the sentence (parents are the active subjects) whilst 'an allowance' has connotations of pocket money. Some students clearly feel uncomfortable with this. Sarah continues:

> I don't like asking from my family because, well, it's their money and my youngest sister stays with them as well, so it seems unfair taking money from them that they could be using on her when she's got to go through it.[7]

The sense here of it being 'their' money and that the student would be 'taking money from them' suggests a desire for independence and control of her own financial affairs.

It could be argued that today's financially, and at times emotionally, dependent student is not new. In many ways the notion of the independent university student was an historical anomaly and current trends merely revert society back to a long-standing status quo. Prior to the Family Law Reform Act of 1969, British youngsters did not reach the Age of Majority until they were 21. Universities held a legal position of *in loco parentis* over the students in their care. The combined effect of lowering the legal age of majority and the introduction of maintenance grants to cover accommodation and living expenses allowed youngsters at university in the 1970s and 1980s to experience a (historically short-lived) glimpse of freedom from parental financial control – although this did not apply to youngsters from wealthier families, and those from less wealthy backgrounds merely traded dependence on parental subsidy for dependence on a state benefit.

Yet what is happening in universities today is qualitatively new and not just a reversion to an earlier era. Prior to 1969, there is little to suggest that parents themselves expected to receive a service, as such, from the institutions attended by their offspring. Prior to 1969 parents did not assume they had to play a role to ensure their child's academic success or future employability. In short, parents in the past did not think or act as consumers of higher education.

In the UK context, today's debates over who 'foots the bill' most often ignore the fact that no parent, however high their income, is expected to pay large sums of money up front to fund their child's higher education tuition fees. All students are entitled to loans to cover the full cost of their university fees. Repaying the future debt is firmly the responsibility of the 'offspring'. Indeed this shifting of financial burden from parent to child was a key motivator of British government policy: 'These reforms take an important step in the direction of treating students as independent adults at 18. The Graduate Contribution Scheme means that no student need rely on their parents to pay for the cost of their tuition' (DfES, 2003: 92).

Yet, whatever the intention of policy, it certainly seems to be the case that parents feel as if they are paying more towards the costs of their child's education. Much of this may be due to increased costs associated with living away from home. Means-tested maintenance loans can leave wealthier parents picking up bills for living expenses and accommodation. However, research by Claire Callender, Professor of Higher Education Policy at Birkbeck University suggests that the amount of money parents contribute to their child's education is less now than at any other time over the past twenty years (Callender, 2011). Callender suggests that the provision of student loans at a subsidised interest rate that do not have to be paid back until students are in employment and earning a minimum level of income, in effect acts as a financial subsidy to middle-class parents. Before student loans, the means testing for government-funded maintenance grants was far more stringent and so parents earning even a moderate income were expected to contribute towards their children's living expenses. Now many more students qualify for loans to cover both living expenses and tuition fees and the necessity for parents to top up these loans has been reduced.

The crisis of adulthood

The fact that parents do not have to pay large sums of money up front to fund their child's higher education indicates that the emergence of parents as co-consumers in their child's university experience is not just a question of finance alone. As with students themselves, the description of parents as co-consumers is more a description of attitudes and behaviours than a literal financial relationship. A range of social, political and cultural factors, other than just money, encourages parents to see themselves in this role. The trend towards 'infantilisation', for example, positions youngsters as adolescent and not fully mature for an increasingly extended period of time. What is notable about infantilisation is the apparent reluctance of many youngsters to oppose such trends. For example, many grown-up children now stay living in the parental home for longer periods than in recent history, often returning home post-graduation. In the UK it is reported that 25 per cent of men aged 25–30 now live with their parents,[8] and some of this generation of young adults has earned the nickname 'boomerang kids' in reference to the way they might leave home to go to university, but then return to the family home in the early twenties and show little sign of leaving. The authors of *Consumer Kids* note: 'companies that track marketing trends talk of "age compression" and the emergence of "kidults", where adolescence is stretched at both ends and reaches through to later life [...] thirty will be the new twenty-one, the official age when you become an adult, as many will still be living with their parents and will have put off marriage until later' (Mayo and Nairn, 2009: 16).

It would be easy to explain these trends as a result of financial constraints – student loan debt combined with poor employment prospects and high house prices may make it difficult for youngsters to strike out on their own. Young adults living in the parental home is not a historically novel concept.

However, what it represent in today's context is a cultural break from the 1960s when aspirations for freedom and independence made many young adults determined to leave home even if it meant living in shared rooms or poor quality accommodation. The aspiration for adulthood meant young adults would often take any work so as to be able to afford a minimum rent or, if living at home, would contribute a proportion of their wages to the household budget. Today's young adults may express a desire for independent living, but the desire is not always strong enough to encourage them to forego the luxuries of the parental home.

Writers on consumer society blame capitalist markets, and more specifically advertisers, for the apparent infantilisation of young adults, as they see it as in the interests of business to keep consumers in a state of perpetual childhood, slaves to their latest impetuous desires. Benjamin Barber, author of *Consumed*, suggests markets and merchandisers seek 'to encourage adult regression, hoping to rekindle in grown-ups the tastes and habits of children so that they can sell globally the relatively useless cornucopia of games, gadgets, and myriad consumer goods for which there is no discernible "need market" other than the one created by capitalism's own frantic desire to sell' (Barber, 2008: 7). Barber locates infantilisation as both a cause and effect of capitalist triumphalism.

Other writers suggest the opposite – that infanilisation is a result not of the triumph of capitalism but the crisis in capitalist societies. When capitalism has nothing to define itself against, and is unable to confidently assert a drive to make a profit for its own sake, the result is political uncertainty as to what it means to act as an autonomous individual, to assume responsibility for one's self, and more significantly, for others: 'it was only when grown-ups stopped believing in adulthood that young people followed suit' (Calcutt, 1999: 157). The concept of being an adult and all it entails is less attractive in a political climate where 'governments treat citizens as vulnerable subjects [...] who tend not to know what is in their best interests' (Furedi, 2005: 142).

If we return briefly to the starting point of this book – that education is a passing-on of the collective wisdom of society from one generation to the next – it follows that teaching (indeed being an adult) inherently assumes a sense of responsibility to past and future generations. Hannah Arendt notes that: 'The teacher's qualification consists in knowing the world and being able to instruct others about it, but his authority rests on his assumption of responsibility for that world' (Arendt, 1954: 186). Today some teachers can at times appear reluctant to accept responsibility for a child's education, as a result of lacking a confident belief in the purpose of their role in relation to either subject knowledge or society more broadly. They may find it difficult to assert what to teach or even how to teach. This is sometimes demonstrated in the greater prominence given to the role parents play in their children's education (and conversely, the diminished impact teachers are perceived to have upon a child's educational development).

Today's primary school classrooms are no longer the preserve of the teacher; schools routinely put a great deal of effort into encouraging parents to play an active role in their child's education, such as setting homework tasks that cannot be completed by the child alone but require adult input. In addition, many primary schools now employ Family Liaison Officers with the specific remit of bringing parents into a relationship with schools. Evidence is frequently cited to support arguments that a child's academic success (or failure) is considered to be primarily due to the actions of parents.[9] In America, Michigan Department for Education publishes a 'factsheet' for parents on the relationship between parental involvement and academic success, which claims: 'The more intensely parents are involved, the more beneficial the achievement effects.'[10] Yet others argue that 'the scientific evidence, when properly weighed, indicates that parents are not as influential nor as powerful in terms of their children's development and future as they are credited for – or as they are blamed for when things go wrong' (Ambert, 1997: 237). It is argued that evidence is used to reflect researchers' assumptions of 'parental determinism' where parents are held to be responsible for almost every aspect of a child's character.[11]

If parents believe that their child's success or failure as an adult depends entirely upon their actions as parents, then being intensely involved in the life of their child appears more of a benevolent duty than in any way problematic, and it is not a duty parents seek to rescind as their children get older. It is presented in mainstream newspapers as a demonstration of parental commitment: 'to find out when the UCAS deadlines were, to prompt and to listen' (Moorhead, 2009). It is perhaps only logical that parents expect to continue playing a 'hands-on' role in their child's education once their child is at university; especially as such behaviour is often affirmed rather than challenged by institutions.

Since the British Conservative government's 1980 Education Act, parents have been encouraged to exercise consumer choice when actively selecting primary and secondary schools for their children from an educational 'market-place'. Such parents are now reluctant to see the process of choosing a university as any different. More parents attend university open days nowadays to the extent that it has become increasingly rare to see a young potential student at a university open day unaccompanied by one or both parents and possibly siblings too. At university open days parents are keener to ask questions of course tutors than are their children, the potential students, leading some universities such as the University of Bristol to set up a 'parents' programme' specifically to answer the concerns and queries of parents (Moorhead, 2009). Most universities now have information on their websites specifically aimed at parents. Lecturers come to expect and to prepare answers for the questions and concerns of parents.

The behaviour and attitudes of parents towards their children once at university has also changed, as parents are less inclined to take a back seat. Parents are described in newspaper articles, often written by exasperated university lecturers, as 'helicopters' hovering over their grown-up offspring, or 'lawn-mowers' mowing down every obstacle in the way of their child's success (Jafar, 2012). When students arrive at university parents stay around for longer than was previously the norm, sometimes remaining with students in their halls of residence so they can reassure themselves that the students are capable of looking after themselves away from home. The University of the West of England reports 'parents overstaying their welcome by staying in the halls of residence' (Coughlan, 2009). Parents may order supermarket food deliveries for their children or pick up mobile phone bills so they have a means of keeping in touch. Such close relationships are often encouraged by universities. The University of Wisconsin-Madison suggests to parents: 'Surprise your student with a care-package from UW Housing Dining and Culinary Services. Choose from birthday cakes, gift certificates, cookies, healthy fruit and snack bags, and studying packages.'[12]

Parents also expect to know how their children are performing academically and will contact course tutors for information as to how their child is getting on. Afshan Jafar, assistant professor of sociology at Connecticut College, notes an increase in the contact academics have with parents: 'They call about final grades [...] they call about extensions on assignments, they call about adding a class late, and they call about their kids not being able to get onto the course they want' (Jafar, 2012). Parents of students at British universities are similarly happy to phone up academic support services on behalf of their children to make appointments for them to attend workshops and one-to-one tutorials to improve their performance. If it is thought to be the case that *other* parents are phoning up course tutors or attending interviews with their children, then all parents assume that this is what they should be doing and that they will not be modelling the conduct of a good parent if they do not act in this way.

It can become the case that if sufficient numbers of parents are behaving as consumers and playing a more dominant role in the university education of their child, then this is what becomes expected. Just as the 'good' student is the one who completes evaluation forms and sits on feedback committees, so the 'good' parent is the one who monitors their child's progress in applying to university and whilst at university. Taken together, these trends encourage both children and parents to consider childhood as a prolonged period extending into the university years, with parents entitled to be involved in decision-making and checking progress. What is perhaps more surprising is that students often do not react against parents behaving in this way but rather expect or welcome it. Students at university who have been used to their parents helping with their school work, contacting teachers on their behalf, arranging their social lives, cooking and cleaning for them may expect this to continue whilst at university and rather than seeing parents contacting their tutors as unwarranted interference in their lives may actually welcome it – or at very least accept it as just the way things are.

University becomes, for many students, a continuation of adolescent life in the parental home rather than a chance to assume independence. This can be seen most literally in the increase in students choosing to attend university close to the parental home so they can return there each evening and do not have to make the transition to leaving home. In the academic year 2010/2011, 19 per cent of all undergraduate students lived at home, up from just 8 per cent in 1984 (cited in Tobin, 2011). For some less wealthy, or more debt-averse, families the prohibitive costs associated with moving away for university will encourage students to remain living at home. However, for an increasing number of students, lack of money is not the key motivator in the decision to remain living at home; it is rather that they prefer the convenience, security and familiarity. Hannah Elder, a twenty-year-old student from Bournemouth University reports as a 'plus-point' the fact that her mother does the cooking, and twenty-year-old Susan Garfirth from Northampton University says, 'After a long day at uni I can come home and cook myself a nice meal, then go to bed without worrying about fire alarms going off at three in the morning' (cited in Tobin, 2011).

As Harold Silver discusses, the provision of residential accommodation by universities has historically been about more than just 'somewhere to live'. It often served an academic and even moral purpose as part of a self-conscious attempt on behalf of institutions to shape adult identity (Silver, 2004: 124). For universities to hold such views necessitated a clear belief in their mission in relation to the moral characteristics a liberal education would acculturate in future generations. Such beliefs in character formation are often derided as elitist nowadays and appropriate only for a time when a small proportion of the population attended university. Today universities provide some students with 'somewhere to live' and the mission, if it indeed it can be described as such, relates less to character formation and more to welfare. University residential accommodation provides parents with reassurance that their children are being looked after whilst living away from home for the first time.

Cultivating dependency

Silver explores the historical mission of the university in shaping the moral, social and cultural character of the emergent adult. Such an institutional role appeared as a natural by-product of the liberal educational agenda but was reinforced by the legal requirement that universities were, until 1969, placed in a position of *in loco parentis* over their students. Such legislation meant that young female students at Oxford University in the first decades of the twentieth century were expected to be accompanied by a chaperone whenever they left the university buildings and night-time curfews were placed upon all students (Robinson, 2009: 50). Such regulations reflected a distinctively moral code but also hinted at the disciplinary role played by universities. Today, universities lack such a distinct mission in relation to moral character formation and there is no legal obligation upon them to act in place of parents.

What has replaced *in loco parentis* is an institutional 'duty of care' which is more about meeting the demands of parents that their children will be well looked after than meeting historical, social, cultural and educational obligations. Professor Rick Trainor, President of Universities UK, notes that: 'Universities have a duty of care to our consumers, our students, and it's in our interest that we tend to their concerns' (Lipsett, 2008). The assumption of a duty of care arguably has far more insidious an impact on eroding emerging adult autonomy than did *in loco parentis* legislation. In the past, students had distinct sets of rules to fight against and spent time devising ingenious methods for circumventing restrictions upon their freedom Jane Robinson in her history of women students notes that although 'transgression meant at least a heavy fine, and possibly suspension, there were ways round the rules' (Robinson, 2009: 181). A duty of care is far more ambiguous and far more difficult for students to argue against, as it is bound up in notions of well-being, mental health and protection. Such a focus on welfare is expected by both government and parents: 'We believe it is reasonable for students and their parents to expect higher education institutions to make student welfare a priority and encourage universities and colleges to work with their students' union to ensure a good range of services' (BIS, 2011: 35). Louise Morley notes that if the relationship between the university and students is one of 'customer' and 'service provider' universities may have to exercise a degree of 'customer care' (see Morley, 2003). In many respects 'duty of care' has come to be the customer service product sold to parents. Although students fought against *in loco parentis* restrictions upon their freedom – or at least devised ways to subvert the rules – it is more difficult for them to argue against customer care.

For some students, especially those living in halls of residence, the university's exercising of its duty of care can be experienced as restrictive. Louisa, a first-year history student, describes what happens when the fire alarm goes off in her hall of residence:

> When we go outside and we're trying to find out whether it's a real fire [...] now we just assume it's a fake one it goes off so often. People don't even bother coming out any more. We ask the Campus Watch people 'What's going on? What's going on?' It does kind of feel like they're the teachers or something; they're the adults looking after us little children.[13]

The tension here between appearing to live independently, yet at the same time experiencing a dependence upon university staff for information, is explicit. The language Louisa uses here suggests the 'Campus Watch' people are like 'teachers' in that they are in authority and have the information the students seek. Teachers are normally associated with schools rather than universities; in this way Louisa comes to position herself and her peers as 'us little children'. Yet as such customer care exercises are bound up in health and safety and presented as for the benefit of the student it is very hard for such conventions to be challenged.

One reason for this lack of challenge is that the effect of schooling and culture upon children means many of today's students have grown up with an assumption of themselves as vulnerable and in need of protection from myriad life pressures and problems. This makes conceptualising their own independence problematic. As touched upon in the previous chapter, in order to exercise individual autonomy, students must have some sense of themselves as actors or 'agents' in the world: resilient in the face of change, capable of influencing their environment and contributing to the society they inhabit. Infantilised students who do not have such a firm belief in themselves as resilient, capable actors need little encouragement to see themselves instead as vulnerable, fragile and in need of support. Some students may enter university already with a sense of confronting a threatening experience and one that they may not be able to cope with (Ecclestone and Hayes, 2009).

Instead of universities challenging the idea that new (particularly intellectual) experiences are stressful and daunting, they often reinforce these notions through the proliferation of institutional mechanisms for providing emotional, practical and academic support (Ecclestone and Hayes, 2009). The intention seems to be that through such support services, students can access a tangible product and emerge satisfied from their experience of university. One example of this is the previously discussed description of what happens when the fire alarm goes off in the halls of residence. The students are left feeling that university representatives are 'the adults looking after us little children'. As Kathryn Ecclestone and Dennis Hayes argue, a therapeutic focus on self-esteem in the classroom has taken hold, in response to an assumption that students are living in uncertain times and need education to help them to cope with experience of anxiety.[14] This almost psychological purpose to education appears attractive to academics reluctant to buy into the discourse of individual human capital. Yet there is a danger that the therapeutic shift in education may be destructive of academic autonomy as the knowledge basis upon which it depends is replaced instead by a focus upon emotion, feelings and personal transformation.

Vulnerable consumers

Therapeutic education, when combined with a duty of care, can mean that instead of helping to promote adult autonomy, universities can serve to reinforce the infantilisation of students. The treatment of students as consumers enhances these trends. One example of this can be seen in the actual process of paying tuition fees as it operates in England in 2012. The present system of tuition fees and loans distances students from the fee-paying process. Twenty-one-year-old psychology student Sam comments:

> You get a letter from the student loans company saying that they've granted you this amount and that kind of thing so when you look at the letter saying £3250, it doesn't even mean that much. If it was sort of in my account first and then I spent it, it would feel like a lot more money. At the moment it's easy to forget about it.[15]

And Melissa adds:

> The only way you really know [how much debt you have] is by looking at the website to see how much the tuition fees are. It's just a bit bizarre the fact that you don't really know where it's come from or what's happening with it.[16]

Students know they are taking out loans to pay university fees and this could, arguably, enhance their sense of personal responsibility as they are responsible for taking out the loan and committed to paying it back. However the process by which money goes directly from the Student Loan Company to the university serves to distance the student from the act of fee-paying.

For some students the need to take out loans and the fear of future debt is experienced as stressful and there is a perception that students need to be supported to cope with the stress of being a consumer. Such assumptions emerge in part from the pre-existing discourse that constructs children as vulnerable to the workings of the capitalist market. Books such as *Consumer Kids, Consumed: How markets corrupt children, infantilise adults and swallow citizens whole*, and *Consuming Life* portray children as exploited children by big business intent upon accessing their pocket money or harnessing children's 'pester power' as a means to their parents' bank balances: 'This pressure can play on teenage vulnerabilities in terms of self-esteem and self-image' (Mayo and Nairn, 2009: 19). The image this creates is of young people as uniquely vulnerable to marketing, advertising and exploitation. It suggests young people are naïve and irrational: 'Children today are cogs in a great, spinning commercial wheel' (Mayo and Nairn, 2009: xv).

When HE is presented as just another product, student-consumers are seen as vulnerable to persuasion, naïve and gullible to the claims made by institutions. This does much to construct students as victims of the exploitative marketing techniques employed by universities. They are presented as unable to defend their own interests and in need of protection from consumer-champions who can expose the workings of the market and reveal the sources of exploitation to young people. According to this argument the demand for tuition-fees turns higher education into one more product vying for the teenage purse and universities into another potentially exploitative marketer to be avoided. In America, students are included as consumers in the remit of pressure groups which lobby on their behalf for a better service; and federal and state officials have acted to protect student consumers. There is an assumption that students need protection from the higher education market just like children exposed to the marketing of McDonalds.

In reality, despite the beliefs of some activists, many students, as young adults, are not uniquely vulnerable consumers but are actually quite market-savvy. They 'arrive as fee-paying customers knowing how to "play" markets to maximise self-interest. They are well-versed in the pseudo-sovereignty status afforded them by broader consumer culture. Their experiences in commercial marketplaces and their confidence as consumers, allow them to carry the same attitudes over to public goods such as education' (Molesworth, Nixon and Scullion, 2009: 279). It might be added that lecturers are not all out to corrupt, persuade, influence and above all else to sell a product.

Conclusions

Universities have traditionally played a role in managing the transition of students to adulthood. When the purpose of a university was perceived in predominantly more liberal terms of promoting knowledge and learning essentially for its own sake, the process of managing the transition to adulthood was bound up in a moral concept of character formation. Universities self-consciously tried to create future social, cultural and political elites. Today's mass HE sector with its focus upon ensuring students receive an employability 'return' upon their tuition-fee 'investment' no longer seeks to play such a role. Students arrive at university less excited at the prospect of embarking upon an intellectual journey and more anxious at the prospect of living away from home.

Universities, in seeking to provide a marketable product to parent-consumers, focus on customer care packages. Lecturers seeking to challenge the dominant 'skills for employability' ideology tend to focus upon the subjective and the emotive sphere, a therapeutic rather than a rigorously academic education. Instead of managing the transition to adulthood, universities seek to safeguard and protect the physical and emotional welfare of students, removing all element of social or educational risk. For some students this means they leave university as childlike as when they started.

Endnotes

1 Higher Education Statistics Agency (http://www.hesa.ac.uk/index. php?option=com_content&task=view&id=1974&Itemid=278) [accessed 28/07/12].

2 http://www.uarts.edu/about/student-consumer-information [accessed 28/07/12].

3 http://www.collegeparents.org/members/resources/articles/ students-%E2%80%93-and-parents-%E2%80%93-are-consumers-american-higher-education [accessed 28/07/12].

4 http://www.timeshighereducation.co.uk/story.asp?storycode=416730 [accessed 28/07/12].

5 Interview with Joanna Williams.

6 Interview with Joanna Williams.

7 Interview with Joanna Williams.

8 Office for National Statistics December 2009.

9 See, for example, Steinberg, L., Elmen, J. and Mounts, N. (1989); Finn, J. D. and Rock, D. A. (1997); Schneider, B. and Lee, Y. (2009)

10 http://www.michigan.gov/documents/Final_Parent_Involvement_Fact_Sheet_14732_7.pdf [accessed 28/07/12].

11 See, for example, Skolnick A. S. and Skolnick J. H. (1994); Lee, E. (28/08/11) in *Spiked-Online*. [accessed 28/07/12].

12 http://www.housing.wisc.edu/parents [accessed 28/07/12].

13 Interview with Joanna Williams.

14 See, for example, Barnett, R. (2007).

15 Interview with Joanna Williams.

16 Interview with Joanna Williams.

7

Beyond entitlement

This book has explored the ways in which students are constructed as consumers of higher education through fee-paying: government policies; media representations of what it means to be a student; lecturers and institutional approaches; school teachers; and advice and guidance counsellors. Yet despite all these mechanisms by which students come to think of themselves as consumers, it remains the case that learning, and education cannot be bought. In paying for higher education students may purchase a service, or a product, but this is not education. As the American academic Michael Potts correctly indicates: 'If higher education loses the idea that other ends are to be subsumed under the internal good of imparting knowledge to students, then it does not deserve to be called "education", much less "higher education"' (Potts, 2005: 61).

In packaging a purchasable commodity for students to consume, universities come to be concerned with many 'other ends' besides 'the internal good of imparting knowledge'. University is sold to parents as a safe and protected environment for their youngsters and as a financial investment in their child's future employability. University is marketed to students as a satisfactory experience in the short term which may, in the long term, increase their earning potential or, perhaps in some instances, have a bearing upon personal projects of individual transformation. The university product is marketed to governments as a means of promoting social inclusion and social justice through a concern with widening participation to disadvantaged social groups, and as a means of supporting the national economy and promoting international competitiveness.

The focus for much marketing is the investment potential of a university experience. This reduces higher education to employability skills that students can trade in the post-graduation labour market for future earnings. As discussed in Chapter Four, the qualitative and quantitative impact of skills training fundamentally shifts the perceived purpose of today's university. In the past, vocational courses such as medicine or law sat alongside other non-instrumental educational options. This meant that vocational courses were placed in a liberal context. There was a clear concept of what it meant to be an educated individual and, as Cardinal Newman argues in his book *The Idea of a University*, it was thought that students would make potentially better doctors or lawyers precisely because of this liberal context to their studies (Newman, 1852). Now liberal courses have been vocationalised as a result not just of changes in the economy but also, importantly, because of changes in the concept and value of knowledge itself.

As Derek Bok argues, money-making activities by universities can be attributed to a broader lack of purpose (Bok, 2003). The intellectual vacuum and lack of clear mission have in part been created by the post-modern challenge to the concept of knowledge itself. The idea that it is possible to understand the world has, in many strands of both academic and public life, been superseded by the idea that the best we can do is to 'complicate' existing assumptions. In the same vein, the notion that culture should preserve and transmit 'the best that has been thought and said' attracts suspicion, as it is regarded as an apology for historical elitism, racial and sexual oppression, and other forms of inequality and abuse. Yet when the concept of knowledge itself is challenged, education cannot be defined and defended as the passing on of knowledge to future generations.

Bok suggests that, having lost sight of any clear mission beyond a vague commitment to excellence, 'our sprawling multiversities are charged with creating a vacuum into which material pursuits have rushed unimpeded' (Bok, 2003: page 5). This intellectual vacuum has been filled by other projects such as employability, social inclusion or personal transformation. As a focus on students' future careers has become the centrepiece of the university, lecturers are removed from any responsibility of asserting what they think it is important for students to know or even particular books that they consider students of a particular discipline should have read (Bloom, 1987). The onus for determining course content is shifted away from lecturers and onto students who are expected to make a career choice (preferably before entering the university) and then to use their time at university in preparing for that career. Bauman argues that the promotion of employability through education is about transforming students (as consumers) into products, or perhaps 'brands', the sum of their human capital: 'they are simultaneously, promoters of commodities and the commodities they promote. They are, at the same time, the merchandise and their marketing agents, the goods and their travelling sales people' (Bauman, 2007: 6).

This focus on employability skills ensures that HE is considered as an investment in the self, irrespective of whether the money comes into universities from the state, private enterprise or the tuition fees of individual students and their families. Universities may still offer something called 'education' but it is less concerned with advancing human knowledge than it is with employability skills. Potts suggests 'if a self-proclaimed university gave up the goal of advancing universal knowledge, it would lose its identity as a university, even if it continued to carry the name "university"' (Potts, 2005: 59). The problem with this, as Bloom indicated, is that 'The student gets no intimation […] that a different and more human way of life can be more harmoniously constructed by what he is going to learn' (Bloom, 1987: 337).

One more radical alternative to the promotion of employability skills is the presentation of HE as concerned with individual projects of personal transformation. Individual development in the form of personal transformation appears to come closest to traditional concepts of education but it is precisely the focus on the self that prevents this from being the same as the universal advancement of knowledge. Personal transformation projects are necessarily individualised and do not present a unifying vision of the world and knowledge. They are relativised: everyone's personal transformation will be different and the quality or extent of a student's personal transformation cannot be objectively judged. A focus on personal transformation often becomes therapeutic in nature, concerned with students' self-esteem and emotions; their feelings in relation to the subject matter they encounter become more important than the mastery of particular content. Within the context of students being constructed as consumers, projects of personal transformation will always be limited because the logic of perceiving students to be consumers, or customers of a university, is that having paid tuition fees, students should receive some form of satisfactory service and cannot be expected to engage in processes of potentially uncomfortable intellectual struggle.

As rigorous academic challenge is abandoned in favour of more instrumental goals, so too is any particular project to encourage the next generation of adults to share, and further develop, society's collectively held knowledge. It is education, in the form of the knowledge gained that is transformative, not the focus on the self or the emotional journey towards achieving this knowledge. True liberal education is transformational in that it requires that the students' whole lives be radically changed by what they have learnt; this may affect their actions, tastes, and choices. Liberal education puts everything a student has previously held to be true at risk of re-examination.

British academics Rajani Naidoo and Iain Jamieson argue that students who internalise a consumer identity in effect place themselves outside of the intellectual community (Naidoo and Jamieson, 2005: 272). They are more likely to resist processes of transformation and perceive themselves as passive consumers of higher education. In promoting personal development and transformation as a product, with the consequent expectation of customer satisfaction, it becomes just one more thing for a university to market. It is irrelevant whether the product is one that is in keeping with liberal sympathies, such as therapeutic projects of self-transformation, or one that appears ruthlessly neo-liberal in intent, such as the transformation of the self into a commodity. None of the products a university promotes, not satisfaction, skills nor personal transformation, is the same as education. In the sense that universities exchange these various products for money, universities have become businesses; businesses that have largely given up on the goal of education as it has traditionally been understood as advancing universal knowledge.

The distancing of universities from education began before students in England were expected to pay tuition fees and before the more recent steep tuition fee increases in American universities. One reason for the removal of education from universities is governments attempting to meet social and political objectives through the sphere of education. As Chapter One of this book explored, governments have long since attempted to meet political objectives through the realm of higher education. Since the inception of the majority of universities we have today, there has been tension between liberal academic goals and more instrumental vocational goals related to the presumed needs of the national economy and the drive for international economic competitiveness. Since the early decades of the last century, there has also been an increasingly explicit political expectation that universities will play a social role: providing graduates for socially useful roles such as teachers and doctors; producing socially engaged citizens; disseminating the culture that will cohere society; or, more recently, providing opportunities for individual social mobility. In taking universities beyond concerns with education for its own sake, such a social role provides as instrumental a sense of purpose for higher education as more explicitly economic objectives.

Yet in recent years something has changed. In the past, these explicitly instrumental goals were in tension with the more liberal goals of the university – the belief that education was important for its own sake and did not need an instrumental justification of either a social or economic sort. A century's-worth of arguments between the supporters of liberal and vocational education bear testament to this being the case. Nowadays, liberal and vocational purposes of education are no longer pitched against each other; instead, one instrumental purpose competes against another. Arguments might rage between academics as to the worth of particular goals, with the politically radical supporters of widening participation to disadvantaged social groups appearing to be defiantly opposed to the neo-liberal exponents of human capital theory. However, all of these political goals come together in a focus upon social mobility. There are few today who argue the case for education for its own sake, education without any purpose at all other than the passing on and development of knowledge and the (often deferred) personal satisfaction to be gained from learning.

The recent focus on social mobility arises from the linking of higher-level educational qualifications to employment prospects, and ultimately to income. Indeed, this relationship between qualification and wealth, or social class, appears to assume the status of common sense. It is also perhaps a relationship that people *want* to believe is true: there is reassurance in the belief that application and effort in education are financially rewarded. American entrepreneur Peter Thiel suggests: 'Education may be the only thing people still believe in in the United States. To question education is really dangerous. It is the absolute taboo. It's like telling the world there's no Santa Claus' (Miller, 2011). Thiel has recently funded youngsters to drop out of college and begin their own businesses instead; he is seeking to demonstrate that the ability to become wealthy is not solely dependent upon education.

Indeed, the precise nature of the relationship between education, employment and wealth is problematic. Although on an individual level it may well be the case that qualifications lead to better employment, it does not follow that this same relationship can be reproduced throughout the whole of society. It is not at all clear whether wealthy individuals have well-paid employment because they are well-qualified, or whether it is their middle-class background that is credentialised and then reproduced through the education system. Similarly, as Alison Wolf argues in *Does Education Matter?*, the role universities play in social mobility may be less to do with any specific knowledge or skills students have gained and more to do with a complex system of ranking and grading the population. If high-paying jobs are limited in number then employers will seek a way of rationing applicants and higher education qualifications provide a useful screening device (Wolf, 2002). An increased number of graduates in society does not in and of itself enhance economic productivity or create employment opportunities where none exist. It only necessitates the bar for rationing applicants be raised higher. This can be seen to be the case in the UK where a degree alone no longer guarantees applicants will even be considered for some graduate employment opportunities. Instead, many companies will now specify that applicants must hold a degree at least at 2.1 level or above.

The goal of promoting social mobility through education has become deeply entrenched as part of a broader politicisation of education and of higher education in particular. The explicitly political approaches adopted by educational researchers have influenced teachers and lecturers as well as policymakers. As far back as 1883, American sociologist John Lester Ward argued in his book *Dynamic Sociology* that education could be an 'essential force in progress' and was associated with 'human betterment'(quoted in Bernbaum, 1977: 17). Writing at the end of the nineteenth century, American philosopher and educationalist John Dewey linked education to democracy and argued that social reform should take place through the social interaction found in schools (Dewey, 1916). British Professor of Education Michael Young notes that by the 1950s much sociology of education was based upon 'the sentiments of Fabian socialism' and that the primary questions raised by the sociology of education related to the promotion of equality of educational opportunity (Young, 1971). By the 1970s social justice through the provision of equal educational opportunity was explicitly linked to the concept of economic efficiency and growth, and British sociologist of education Gerald Bernbaum noted: 'at an individual level education can be seen as the key to social mobility' (Bernbaum, 1977: 25).

In the 1970s arguing for social justice through the provision of educational opportunity appeared as a radical critique of an HE sector which still catered for a comparatively small and select proportion of the population in the context of an economic downturn and high levels of unemployment. This argument also appeared in radical opposition to the exponents of human capital theory. Since the mid–1990s, however, the concerns of educational researchers, universities and government policy makers have increasingly coincided as the social purpose of HE has come to the fore.

Since this time, successive British government policies have stated an intention for universities to play a role in ensuring social justice as part of, not instead of, a more overtly economic focus upon skills for employability. Upon its election in 1997, the British Labour government made the promotion of social inclusion, which was most frequently equated with being in employment, a political priority. This led to a shift towards vocational instrumentalism in all forms of post-compulsory education. In the later years of the Labour administration this became a more explicit focus upon individual social mobility – a motivation for HE that has been shared by the succeeding coalition government. Instead of the belief that education is to serve a social and an economic purpose, encapsulated for the individual in social mobility, appearing as a radical challenge to elitist and academically autonomous universities, all sides now appear to agree that this is the main purpose of the sector.

Despite political changes, the form that the focus upon social mobility consistently takes in practice is the enactment of policies and initiatives designed to promote widening participation. Universities have been prompted not just to increase the overall numbers of students but more specifically to recruit students considered to be from more disadvantaged backgrounds in a political attempt at engineering a more just society. Some initial statement of intent to widen participation dates from the G.I. Bill in the United States and from the Robbins Report in the UK. As discussed in Chapter One, Baron Lionel Robbins in 1963 expressed his concern that a place at university should be made available to all children who had the potential to benefit from higher education irrespective of their social class.[1] This could broadly be caricatured as a meritocratic approach to widening participation. Post-Robbins, early attempts at widening participation succeeded in increasing the number of students in universities (community colleges or polytechnics) overall, primarily through expanding the number of middle-class students. This led to colloquial criticism that such attempts at widening participation succeeded only in establishing universities as 'finishing schools' for the middle-classes as they simply provided for doctors' daughters as well as sons (Morley, 2011).

More recently there has been a shift from universities being encouraged to select the brightest children from all social classes to participate in an academically, if not socially elite learning environment, to a focus on widening participation as an end in itself. A 2003 British policy document notes: 'We see all HEIs excelling in teaching and reaching out to low participation groups, coupled with strengths in one or more of research; knowledge transfer; linking to the local and regional economy; and providing clear opportunities for students to progress' (DfES, 2003b: 26). What is interesting in this sentence is not so much the statement of aims of higher education but the order in which they are presented. Whereas in the past, teaching and research may have been considered the core aims of a university and other aims incidental or certainly less significant, this sentence places 'teaching and reaching out to low-participation groups' as the core objectives and research appears to be an additional extra. Here we see a significant shift in emphasis away from recruiting academically able students irrespective of class background. Now universities are to be judged on their ability to attract students from lower socio-economic backgrounds largely irrespective of their academic or intellectual ability to benefit from higher education. Such widening participation activity is now considered a key function of universities.

The problem for higher education is that when widening participation, as an end in itself, becomes a key goal of the university there is little sense of what people are being recruited to participate in and, perhaps more importantly, why. In 1963 there was an assumption not just that universities had something to offer bright youngsters, but that such students, through their presumed contribution to the development of knowledge, had something to offer first their universities and then broader society. This was clearly about more than just youngsters making a financial contribution to the university in the form of tuition fees paid to the institution on their behalf by the local authority; rather it was assumed that students would contribute to the intellectual life of their institution and that a more educated population would be for the public good.

At the time there was some consensus on what it meant both to be generally educated, and to have mastered a body of knowledge associated with particular academic disciplines. In suggesting university should be for the brightest irrespective of social class background, Robbins was seeking to move away from the idea that access to higher education was an entitlement for children from wealthier, more privileged social class backgrounds. Robbins suggested access to higher education had to be earned not through wealth but through proven commitment to academic study as demonstrated through educational success prior to entering a university.

Since the late 1990s emphasis has shifted from merely increasing participation in total across the system as a whole, to a specific focus upon recruiting students from lower social class backgrounds with less emphasis placed upon students demonstrating previously acquired academic ability.

This has been achieved in a number of ways. A regulatory body, the Office For Fair Access (OFFA) was established in 2004 and aims to ensure universities meet targets related to widening participation. Universities are publicly held to account for the number of students from less advantaged social backgrounds that they recruit: 'Performance indicators published by the Funding Council give information on how well each institution recruits low participation groups and how that compares to "benchmarks" based on what would be expected for an institution in similar circumstances, taking the qualifications and background of the applicants into account' (DfES, 2003b: 73).

As British Secretary of State for Business Innovation and Skills, Lord Mandelson urged universities to use 'contextual data' to accept students with lower grade A levels or no A levels at all (Tobin, 2010). This reflects an assumption that it is easier for more socially privileged children, perhaps at private schools, to achieve high-level entry qualifications than their less privileged peers. Such beliefs date from the work of Bail Bernstein and Pierre Bourdieu (Bernstein, 1973; Bourdieu, 1979), who argued that the family circumstances and the socialisation processes experienced by working-class children were key determinants of their future academic success. Yet such views contain a strong element of determinism, presenting people as mere products of their home environment. This denies the potential for youngsters to overcome their personal circumstances through intellectual engagement. It is precisely because knowledge is *not* a commodity that it is accessible to all who are determined to pursue it irrespective of wealth, connections or family circumstances.

Proponents of offering different groups of students different university entrance criteria assume that such measures merely equalise the inherent disadvantages faced by working-class youngsters in the education system. It is argued that social advantage makes it easier for middle-class students to achieve good exam grades and to secure places at top-ranking universities. This suggests that bright working-class students are at an inherent disadvantage and need to be admitted with lower grades so that they can then compete as equals. The current preoccupation with social mobility exacerbates arguments that there should be different entry tariffs. When access to higher education is considered a necessity for both employment and democratic participation, denying individuals access to HE is seen as an infringement upon personal rights. The presentation of HE as fundamental to participation in society means that university is no longer an earned privilege, but has instead come to be conceived of as a 'right' or an entitlement of citizenship, irrespective not only of social class but of academic ability or effort or application. Access to HE is considered an entitlement much in the same way as British citizens would expect to be able to access schools, welfare benefits if unemployed, or the National Health Service if sick or injured.

In this way, universities come to be conceived of as just another service provided by the state to which all should be entitled. Louise Morley notes that the notion of university as concerned with customer care and outcomes, 'entitlements and consumer rights', has 'changed social and pedagogical relations in the academy' (Morley, 2003: 79). It is this sense of entitlement to access HE that helps enshrine students as consumers irrespective of fee-paying. Fee-paying merely enhances the sense that once rights have been fulfilled and access to university secured, three years'-worth of payments and attendance mean students are entitled to a degree product.

Indeed, part of the vehement opposition to increased tuition fees that many people demonstrate is precisely because HE is considered an entitlement. Political activists in America have called for the government and the administrators of loans to forgive student debt. In 2011, this cause won the backing of the Occupy Wall Street movement of protesters who demonstrated against the perceived excesses of the financial sector (Kennard and Bond, 2011). In America, online petitions advocating student loan forgiveness gathered hundreds of thousands of signatures (Vedder, 2011). Yet it is ironic that opposition to individuals paying university tuition fees is greatest at the point in time when HE is most related to individual private benefit in the form of employment prospects and earnings.

Today there is little sense of higher education being an act of scholarship to develop knowledge for the benefit of society. Whilst much debate ensues around whether students should pay for HE or not, and how much they should pay, such debates ignore the issue of what students are being expected to pay *for*. When HE is presented to prospective students at every turn as an investment in their future employability and an investment which can be expected to reap a financial reward in future earnings, then it is difficult to justify students not making a financial contribution towards this end.

However, it could be argued that in being asked to pay for job training and social inclusion, students are in effect being asked to fund nothing more than perceived solutions to an economic and political crisis. When it becomes unprofitable for businesses to invest in training their workforce, or lack of competition means there is little concern that workers will transfer their labour elsewhere, as Zygmunt Bauman notes, the 'task of sustaining the saleability of labour *en masse* is left to the private worries of individual men and women (for instance, by switching the cost of skill acquisition to private, and personal, funds), and they are now advised by politicians and cajoled by advertisers to use their own wits and resources to stay on the market, to increase their market value or not let it drop, and to earn the appreciation of prospective buyers' (Bauman, 2007: 9).

Similarly, in the absence of national governments presenting a coherent, confident political vision for citizens either to buy into or oppose, youngsters are expected to purchase their social inclusion into society through attendance at university. In this sense, universities are filling the gaps left by the crisis in politics and economics. Universities are now expected to provide for what would in the past have been the role of state and markets and the costs associated with this are placed upon students themselves. In this way, university tuition fees come to be about making students pay for the state to provide them with what is necessary for them to participate in society, rather than a university simply offering opportunities to engage in education that individuals can decide to take or leave.

The nature of the market in HE, especially in the UK, is that it is heavily state-regulated. Universities have only limited freedom to set fee levels and to determine student numbers. As already discussed, universities are also under considerable pressure to engineer a specific socially inclusive mix. Universities have accepted this role because for many involved in higher education, funding sources have been fetishised above knowledge content to the extent that being publicly funded, no matter how many conditions are applied or how far away from the purpose of education universities are expected to move, is considered preferable to private funding whether from business sponsorship or private individuals.

Despite such institutional acquiescence to the non-educational objectives of employability and inclusion, it remains the case that for the most part students do not want to be considered as consumers and lecturers do not want to deliver a service. This can serve as a reminder that students and lecturers, as a community of scholars, can be united in the goal of education. As Potts argues, the student-teacher relationship is a relationship among people; 'it is not like the relationship between the salesperson at the local automobile dealership and the customer' (Potts, 2005: 62). Many young people are genuinely excited by their subject choices and seek intellectual challenge from their time at university and are highly critical of implications that they may have somehow 'bought' their degrees (Williams, 2011a; Molesworth, Nixon and Scullion, 2009). This means that universities and individual lecturers can do much to challenge the construction of the student as consumer. A useful starting point is the reinstatement of knowledge content in the university curriculum. Allan Bloom notes that 'Wherever the Great Books make up a central part of the curriculum, the students are excited and satisfied, feel they are doing something that is independent and fulfilling, getting something from the university they cannot get elsewhere. The very fact of this special experience, which leads nowhere beyond itself, provides them with a new alternative and a respect for study itself' (Bloom, 1987: 344). In making the case for quality education, with students and lecturers united as a community of scholars, it can be possible to break down the perceived link between fee-paying and consumption.

When the focus of higher education is upon passing on the knowledge of previous generations for students to engage with and interpret, students may be able to need to make knowledge their own through intellectual risk-taking rather than counting contact hours or ticking off learning outcomes. They can then be encouraged to become independent learners, rather than participating simply as a means of claiming their entitlement.

In this way a university can truly become an academy for the best that has been thought for public benefit. Only then can debates about who pays for higher education and how much become potentially meaningful.

Proposals for change

Skills for employability, personal transformation and social inclusion are all important in their own terms. They are not, however, the same as education. Debates about university tuition fees are meaningless when universities become detached from higher education. There is a danger that society becomes focused on the price of higher education at the same time that it loses sight of its real value. The educational value of attending university urgently needs to be established. Some suggestions for achieving this include:

- We should stop seeing university admission as either an entitlement or as a rite of passage for all youngsters. It should be possible to enter skilled employment and to become a fully democratic citizen without having attended university. This necessitates other employment, educational and training options being made available to youngsters.

- Higher education should be there for anyone who wants to access it irrespective of wealth or family background but based upon genuine and sustained intellectual commitment to engaging in rigorous and challenging academic pursuits.

- Non-vocational higher education disciplines should not focus on employability. This encourages students to see a degree as an instrumental investment and relieves lecturers of the pressure to justify their disciplines in academic terms alone. Those within the academy should be able to make the case for non-vocational education in its own terms.

- Universities should not be held to account for the emotionally arbitrary satisfaction levels of their students. Lecturers should feel confident to remind students that genuinely engaging in intellectual struggle is not intended to be immediately satisfying. The expectation of satisfaction assumes lecturers are to provide a service for students.

- Students and lecturers need to be united in the common goal of developing and interacting with disciplinary knowledge. Too often lecturers and students are presented as being on opposing sides with mutually exclusive interests – lecturers perhaps seeking to protect research time, students to ensure a better service. Learning often depends upon the relationships between lecturers and students and such relationships are prevented from developing if opposition is assumed.

● Lecturers and students need to debate together the purpose of university. The result of meeting short-term employability or satisfaction goals means that higher education too often gets reduced to its most technical parts: assessment feedback returned within a given period of time; emails answered within a set period; or lecture notes made available in advance, for example. These initiatives are absolutely not, even in total, the same as education.

Only when the purpose of education is placed at the heart of the university, rather than job training or social inclusion, can a debate on whether higher education is to be funded from the public or private purse, and how much money it should receive, become truly meaningful.

Endnote

1 Committee on Higher Education (1963).

BIBLIOGRAPHY

ACCM (1987) *Education for the Church's Ministry, The report of the working party on assessment*, ACCM Occasional Paper (22).

AFP (2011) 'Americans worried by soaring tuition fees at colleges' in Al Arabiya News (02/07/11).

Ambert, A-M. (1997) *Parents, Children and Adolescents: interactive relationships and development in context*, New York: The Haworth Press.

Ashley, M. (2011) 'From America, with caution: avoid our higher education mistakes' in *The Independent* (4/05/11).

Ashwin, P., Abbas, A. and McLean, M. (2011) 'A bad deal for 'consumers'' in *Times Higher Education* (18/11/11).

Astin, A. (1991) 'The changing American college student: implications for educational policy and practice' in *Higher Education*, 22.

Arendt, H. (1954) *Between Past and Future*, London: Penguin.

Arum, R. and Roska, J. (2011). *Academically adrift: Limited learning on college campuses*, Chicago: The University of Chicago Press.

Austen, J. (1813) *Pride and Prejudice*, London: Wordsworth Classics.

Bailey, R. (2001) 'Overcoming veriphobia – learning to love truth again' in *British Journal of Educational Studies*, 49 (2).

Barber, B. (2008) *Consumed: How markets corrupt children, infantilise adults and swallow citizens whole*, New York: Norton.

Barnett, R. (2011) 'The marketised university: defending the indefensible' in Molesworth, Nixon and Scullion (eds) *The Marketisation of Higher Education and the Student as Consumer*, London: Routledge.

Barnett, R. (2007) *A Will to Learn: Being a Student in an Age of Uncertainty*, Maidenhead: McGraw-Hill/ Open University Press.

Basu, K. (2011) 'Socratic Backfire?' in *Inside Higher Ed* (31/10/11).

Bauman, Z. (2008) *Consuming Life*, Cambridge: Polity Press.

BBC News (2003) *Clarke Criticised over Classics* http://news.bbc.co.uk/1/hi/education/2712833.stm (31/01/03) [accessed 28/04/11].

Becher, T. and Trowler, P. (2001) *Academic Tribes and Territories: intellectual enquiry and the cultures of disciplines* (2nd edition), Buckingham: Open University Press/SRHE.

Becker, G. (1993) *Human Capital*, Chicago: The University of Chicago Press.

Bekhradnia, B (2009) 'Good University Guide 2010: Counting the hours until graduation' in *The Times* (03/06/09).

Berg, I. (1971) *Education and Jobs: The Great Training Robbery*, Boston: Beacon Press.

Berger, P. and Luckmann, T. (1966) *The Social Construction of Reality*, New York: Anchor Books.

Bernbaum, G. (1977) *Knowledge and Ideology in the Sociology of Education*, London: Macmillan.

Bernstein, B. (1971) *Class, Codes and Control, Volume II, Applied Studies Towards a Sociology of Language*, London: Routledge & Kegan Paul Ltd.

Biesta, G. (2009) *Good Education: What it is and why we need it*. Inaugural lecture at The Stirling Institute of Education: University of Stirling (04/03/09).

BIS (2009) *Higher Ambitions*, London: The Stationery Office.

—(2011) *Higher Education: Students at the Heart of the System*, London: The Stationery Office.

Bishop Grosseteste University College Lincoln (2010) *Student Charter August 2010* in Student Charter Group (2011) *Final Report January 2011* available at: http://www.bis.gov.uk/assets/biscore/higher-education/docs/s/11–736-student-charter-group.pdf [accessed 28/07/12].

Bloom, A. (1987) *The Closing of the American Mind*, New York: Simon and Schuster Inc.

Blunkett, D. (2000) 'Speech on Higher Education delivered at Greenwich Maritime University'. (15/2/20).

Bok, D. (2003) Universities in the Marketplace: The Commercialisation of Higher Education, New Jersey: Princeton University Press.

Bourdieu, P. (1979) *The Inheritors: French Students and Their Relations to Culture*, Chicago: University of Chicago Press.

Bourdieu, P. and Passeron, J. (1990) *Reproduction in Education, Society and Culture*, London, Sage Publications.

Breslauer, G. (2011) 'Letter on university education' in *The Economist* (1/10/11).

Brown, R. (2011) *Higher Education and the Market*, Oxon: Routledge.

—(2010) 'Nonsense on Stilts: The Browne Proposals on Quality' *Thames Valley University Institute for Learning and Teaching Annual Lecture* (3/11/10).

Browne, J. (2010) *Securing a Sustainable Future for Higher Education: An Independent Review of Higher Education Funding and Student Finance*, London: The Stationery Office.

Brzezinski, P. (2010) 'Compared to their American peers, British students have nothing to complain about' in *The Telegraph* (09/12/10).

Calcutt, A. (1999) *White Noise: An A-Z of the contradictions in cyberculture*, New York: Palgrave Macmillan.

Callaghan, J. (15/10/1976) *Towards a National Debate*, Oxford: Ruskin College.

Carpentier V. (2010) 'Public-Private Substitution in Higher Education Funding and Kondratiev Cycles: the impacts on home and international students' in E. Unterhalter and V. Carpentier (eds), *Global Inequalities and Higher Education, Whose Interests Are We Serving?* Houndmills: Palgrave MacMillan.

Carr, D. (2009) 'Revisiting the liberal and vocational dimensions of university education' in *British Journal of Education Studies*, 57 (1).

Chessum, M. (2010) 'Today is our 1968 Moment' in *The Guardian* (09/12/10).

Callender, C. (2011) 'A critical assessment of the government's reforms of student funding – all change or no change?' SRHE seminar held at London Metropolitan University (17/05/11).

Clare J. (2006) 'Lecturers unite in their refusal to dumb down' in *The Telegraph* (12/04/06).

Clark, L. (2009) 'Average student debts will hit more than £10, 000 by the end of the decade' in *The Daily Mail*, (21/04/09).

Collini, S. (2010) 'Browne's Gamble' in *London Review of Books* (02/11/10).

Committee on Higher Education (1963), *Higher education: report of the Committee appointed by the Prime Minister under the Chairmanship of Lord Robbins 1961–63*, London: HMSO.

Cooper, P. (2004) 'The gift of education: An anthropological perspective on the commoditization of learning' in *Anthropology Today* 20 (6).

Coughlan, S. (2009) 'Parents Reluctant to Leave Student Accommodation' http://www.bbc.co.uk/1/hi/8413658.stm BBC News (15/12/09) [accessed 28/07/12].

—(2011) 'Students to get best buy facts and consumer rights', http://www.bbc.co.uk/news/education–13874483 BBC News (24/6/11) [accessed 28/07/12].

Dearing, R. (1997) *Report of the National Committee of Inquiry into Higher Education*, London: The Stationery Office.

Dewey, J. (1916) *Democracy and Education*, New York: Free Press.

DfE (1993) *The Charter for Higher Education*, London: DfE Citizen's Charter.

DfES. (2003a) *The Future of Higher Education*, London: The Stationery Office.

—(2003b) *Widening Participation*, London: The Stationery Office.

DoE (2011) Press Release: *Default Rates Rise for Federal Student Loans: Department continues work to protect taxpayer funds and help students manage their debt* (12/09/11).

Dill, D. (2003) 'Allowing the market to rule: The case of the United States' in *Higher Education Quarterly* 57 (2).

Dinkins, S. (2009) 'The Dreaded Grade Appeal' in *Inside Higher Ed* (08/05/09).

Doughty, S. (2007) 'UK students are "least hard-working in Europe"' in *The Daily Mail* (24/09/07).

Eagleton, T. (2011) A. C. Grayling's Private University is Odious' in *The Guardian* (06/06/11).

Ecclestone, K. and Hayes, D. (2009) *The Dangerous Rise of Therapeutic Education*, London: Routledge.

Epstein, J. (1999) *The Higher Education Amendments*, The HE Center for Alcohol and Other Drug Prevention (June 1999).

Evans, M. (2004) *Killing Thinking: The Death of the Universities*, London: Continuum.

Finn, J. D. and Rock, D. A. (1997) 'Academic Success Among Children at risk for school failure', in *Journal of Applied Psychology*, 82 (2).

Frean, A. (2008) 'Students prefer studying to socialising, says survey' in *The Times* (11/09/08).

Furedi, F. (2004) *Therapy Culture: Cultivating Vulnerability in An Uncertain Age*, London: Routledge.

—(2005) *The Politics of Fear: Beyond Left And Right*, London: Continuum Press.

—(2009a) 'Now is the age of the discontented' in *Times Higher Education* (04/06/09).

—(2009b) *Wasted: Why education isn't educating*, London: Continuum.

—(2011) 'Introduction to the Marketisation of Higher Education and the Student as Consumer' in Molesworth, Nixon and Scullion (eds) *The Marketisation of Higher Education and the Student as Consumer*, London: Routledge.

Garner, R. (2009) 'Why are students complaining so much, and do they have a case?' in *The Independent* (20/05/09).

Grayling, A. C. (2002) 'I'm not a commodity' in *The Independent on Sunday*, (03/11/02).

Grimston, J. (2011) 'Universities to reveal students' job prospects' in *The Times* (26/6/11).

Golan, J. (2011) 'As California State Tuition Rises, Financial Aid Offices Struggle to Adjust' in *The New York Times* (24/09/11).

Gordon, P., Aldrich, R. and Dean, D. (1991) *Education and Policy in England in the Twentieth Century*, London: Woburn Press.

Hardi, J. (2000) 'A new generation's choice isn't Coke', in *Chronicle of Higher Education*, 46 (33).

Harrison, R. (2004) 'Telling stories about learners and learning' in Satterthwaite, J., Atkinson, E. and Martin, W. (eds) *The Disciplining of Education, New Languages of Power and Resistance*, Trentham Books: Stoke on Trent.

Hayes, D. (2009) 'Academic Freedom and the Diminished Subject', *British Journal of Educational Studies*, 57 (2).

Heller, D. 'Foreword' in Brown (2011) *Higher Education and the Market*, Oxon: Routledge.

Hess, F. M. (2011) 'I Owe U: Student Loan Debt Isn't a Big Deal – It's a Good Deal' in *The Daily* (15/04/11)

Higher Education Statistics Agency, *Statistical First Release 153*, available at: http://www.hesa.ac.uk/index.php?option=com_content&task=view&id=1936& Itemid=161 [accessed 28/07/12].

Hill, F. M. (1995) 'Managing service quality in higher education' in *Quality Assurance in Education*, 3 (3) 10–21.

Hobsbawm, E. (1987) *The Age of Empire*, London: Abacus.

Hohendorf, G. (1993) 'Wilhem Von Humboldt' in *Prospects: the quarterly review of comparative education*, vol. XXIII, no. 3/4, 613–23.

House of Commons, Innovation, Universities, Science and Skills Committee (2009) *Students and Universities Eleventh Report of Session 2008–09, Volume I*, London: The Stationery Office.

Hurst, G. and Sugden, S. (2010) 'University Student Charters to tell lecturers they must do better' in *The Times* (01/04/2010).

Husen, T. (1974) *The Learning Society*, London: Metheun.

Illich, I. (1970) *Deschooling Society*, Harmondsworth: Penguin.

Inglis, F. (2011) 'Economical with the Actualite' in *Times Higher Education* (6/10/11).

Institute for College Access and Success, The Project on Student Debt, *Debt Facts and Sources* available at: http://projectonstudentdebt.org/files/File/Debt_Facts_ and_Sources.pdf [accessed 28/07/12].

Jafar, A. (2012) 'Consumerism in higher education: the rise of the helicopter parent in *The Guardian* (08/02/12).

Kaye, T., Bickel, R. and Birtwistle, T. (2006) 'Criticizing the image of the student as consumer: examining legal trends and administrative responses in the US and UK', *Education and the Law*, 18 (2–3) 85–129.

Kennard, M. and Bond, S. (2011) 'US student debt impact likened to subprime crisis' in Financial Crisis' in *The Financial Times* (16/10/11).

Kennedy, H. (1997) *Learning Works*, London: The Stationery Office.

Leach, J. (2006) 'The Informed Choice' in *The Guardian* (02/05/06).

Leathwood, C. and O'Connell P. (2003) "It's a struggle': the construction of the 'new student' in higher education' in *Journal of Education Policy*, 18 (6) 597–615.

Lee, E. (2011) 'The Tyranny of Parental Determinism' at *Spiked-Online*, http://www.spiked-online.com/index.php/site/article/11013/ [accessed 24/02/12].

Lewin, T. (2011) 'Student Loan Default Rates Rise Sharply in Past Year' in *The New York Times* (12/09/11).

Lightfoot, L. (2003) 'Students win their fight for damages' in *The Telegraph* (04/03/03).

Lipsett, A. (2008) 'Let's deal with complaints quickly, says Denham' in *The Guardian* (11/09/08).

Littlejohn, R. (2010) 'Toytown Trots, Twitter and the Trumpton Riots' in *The Daily Mail* (12/11/10).

Locke, W. (2011) 'False Economy? Multiple Markets, Reputational Hierarchy and Incremental Policy Making in UK Higher Education', in Brown (2011) *Higher Education and the Market*, Oxon: Routledge.

MacErlean, N. (2005) 'Future Shock as Degrees bring no profit' in *The Observer* (04/09/05).

Malvern, J. and Woolcock, N. (2008) 'We pay the fees so you supply the mod-cons, students tell universities' in *The Times* (17/11/08).

Mandelson, P. (2009) 'Higher Education and Modern Life', *Birkbeck University Lecture* (27/7/09).

Marcus, J. (2011) 'The Wal-Mart ethos attracts few buyers among US lecturers' in *Times Higher Education* (27/01/11).

Maskell, D. and Robinson, I. (2002) *The New Idea of A University*, Thorverton: Imprint Academic.

Mayo, E. and Nairn, A. (2009) *Consumer Kids. How Big Business is Grooming our Children for Profit*, Constable: London.

McCracken, E. (2011) 'The choice is simple: elite universities or free classes for students. It's time for Scotland to make up its mind' in *The Sunday Herald* (13/2/11).

Mill, J. S. (1867) *Inaugural Address to the University of St. Andrews*, Longmans.

Miller, C. C. (2011) 'Want Success in Silicon Valley? Drop Out of School' in *The New York Times* (25/05/11).

Molesworth, M., Nixon, E. and Scullion, R. (2009) 'Having, being and higher education: the marketisation of the university and the transformation of the student into consumer' in *Teaching in Higher Education* 14 (3) 277–87.

Moorhead, J. (2009) 'Ready for the empty nest?: Open days at university are increasingly catering not just for potential students, but for their parents, too' in *The Guardian* (30/06/09).

Morgan, J. (2011) 'Times Higher Education World Reputation Rankings' in *Times Higher Education* (10/03/11).

Morley, L. (2003) 'Reconstructing students as consumers: power and assimilation?' in Slowey, M. and Watson, D. *Higher Education and The Lifecourse*, London: SRHE and Open University Press.

—(2010) 'Researching Absences and Silences in Higher Education', *Higher Education Close Up 5: Think Pieces*, http://www.lancs.ac.uk/fss/events/hecu5/docs/Morley.pdf [accessed 28/07/12].

Morphew, C. and Taylor, B. J. (2011) 'Markets in the US Higher Education System' in Brown (2011) *Higher Education and the Market*, Oxon: Routledge.

Naidoo, R. and Jamieson, I. (2005) 'Empowering participants or corroding learning? Towards a research agenda on the impact of student consumerism in higher education', *Journal of Education Policy*, 20 (3) 267–381.

Newman, Cardinal J. H. (1959, original 1852) *The Idea of a University*, Image Books: New York.

Newman, M. (2007) 'NUS alarmed by one-sided student contract' in *Times Higher Education* (13/7/07).

New York Times Blogs, http://roomfordebate.blogs.nytimes.com/2010/01/03/are-they-students-or-customers/?gwh=8D1AB71C984502BEC5836660BCEA71C0 [accessed 28/07/12].

Nocera, J. (2011) 'Why We Need For-Profit Colleges' in *The New York Times* (16/09/11).

O'Hear, A. (2001) 'Matthew Arnold' in Palmer, J. (ed.) (2001)*Fifty Major Thinkers on Education*, Routledge: London.

Palmer, G. (2011) 'An American View of Tuition Fees' in *The Spectator* (02/07/11).

Porter, A. (2011) 'Clegg deserves a fair hearing on improving social mobility' in *The Times* (07/04/2011).

Potts, M. (2005) 'The consumerist subversion of education' in *Academic Questions*, 18 (3) 54–64.

Pring, R. (1995) *Closing the Gap Liberal Education and Vocational Preparation.* London: Hodder and Stoughton.

—(2004) *Philosophy of Educational Research*, London: Continuum.

Prosser, M. and Trigwell, K. (1999), *Understanding Learning and Teaching: The experience in higher education*, Open University Press, Malabar, FA.

Pugsley, L and Coffey, A. (2002) *Keeping the "Customer" satisfied: parents in the higher education marketplace*, Welsh Journal of Education, vol. 11, no. 2

Redmond, P. (2009) 'Power Struggle: Who said students today were apathetic? They have simply found new ways to protest and new targets' in *The Guardian* (06/01/09).

Riesman D. (1998) *On Higher Education: The Academic Enterprise in an Era of Rising Student Consumerism*, New Jersey: Transaction Publishers.

Reisz, M. (2011) 'More ferrets, fewer sponges' in *Times Higher Education* (31/3/11).

Robinson, J. (2010) *Bluestockings: The remarkable story of the first women to fight for an education*, London: Penguin.

Roderick, G. and Stephens, M. (1981) *Where did we go wrong? : Industrial performance, education, and the economy in Victorian Britain*, Sussex: Falmer Press.

Ross, A. (2003) 'Higher Education and Social Access: To the Robbins Report' in Archer, Hutchings and Ross (Eds.) (2003) *Higher Education and Social Class: Issues of Inclusion and Exclusion*, London: Routledge.

Ruddick, S. (2006) 'Reason's femininity' in N. R. Goldberger, J. M. Tarule, B. M. Clinchy and M. F. Belenky (eds) *A Case for Connected Knowing. Knowledge, Difference, and Power: essays inspired by women's ways of knowing*, New York: Basic Books.

Sabri, D. (2010) 'Absence of the academic from higher education policy' in *Journal of Education Policy*, 25.

—(2011) 'What's wrong with 'the student experience'?' in *Discourse: Studies in the Cultural Politics of Education*, (32) 5.

Schultz, T. (1971) *Investment in Human Capital*, New York: The Free Press.

Schneider, B. and Lee, Y. (2009) 'A Model for Academic Success: The School and Home Environment of East Asian Students' in *Anthropology and Education Quarterly*, 21 (4).

Scullion, R. Molesworth, M. And Nixon, E. (2011) 'Arguments, responsibility and what is to be done about marketisation' in Molesworth, Nixon and Scullion (eds) *The Marketisation of Higher Education and the Student as Consumer*, Oxon: Routledge.

Skolnick, A. S. and Skolnick, J. H. (1994) *Family in Transition*, New York: Harper Collins.

Senior Lecturer British University, (2011) 'Maintain standards? That's way more than my job's worth' in *Times Higher Education*, (17/3/11).

Shepherd, J. and Williams, R. (2010) 'Student complaints about universities rise steeply' in *The Guardian* (15/06/10).

Singh, G. (2002) 'Educational consumers or educational partners: a critical theory analysis' in *Critical Perspectives on Accounting* (13) 681–700.

Silver, H. (1983) *Tradition and Higher Education*, Winchester: Winchester University Press.

—(2004) 'Residence and accommodation in higher education: abandoning a tradition' in *Journal of Educational Administration and History*, 36 (2)

Slaughter, S. and Leslie, L. (1997) *Academic capitalism: Politics, policies, and the entrepreneurial university*, Baltimore: John Hopkins University Press.

Smith, R. (2001) 'John Locke' in Palmer, J. (ed.) *Fifty Major Thinkers on Education*, Routledge: London.

Smithers, R. (2007) 'Degrees continue to pay off for graduates' in *The Guardian*, (07/02/07).

Smith-Squire, A. (2008) 'The curse of the helicopter mothers who hover over their grown-up children' in *The Daily Mail* (17/01/08).

Staff Reporter (2000) 'The rise and rise of the student as consumer' in *The Independent* (11/05/00).

—(2005) 'Student Moans Adding Up' in *The Times* (23/08/05).

—(2011) 'Excellence for Fewer' in *The Economist* (10/09/11).

Steinberg, L., Elmen, J. D. and Mounts, N. S. (1989) 'Authoritative parenting, psychosocial maturity, and academic success among adolescents' in *Child Development* (60).

Student Charter Group (2011) *Final Report January 2011* available at: http://www.bis.gov.uk/assets/biscore/higher-education/docs/s/11–736-student-charter-group.pdf [accessed 28/07/12].

Sugden, J. (2011) 'Student Complaints Jump by a Third' in *The Times* (14/06/11).

Sugden, J. and Rennison, J. (2011) 'Students lose the taste for rebellion as they reject more demonstrations' in *The Times* (13/04/11).

The White House (1998) *Fact Sheet on Higher Education Amendments of 1998*, Office of the Press Secretary, (10/7/98).

The Project on Student Debt (2010) *Debt Facts and Sources*, http://www.projectonstudentdebt.org/files/File/Debt_Facts_and_Sources.pdf [accessed 28/07/12].

Thomas, L. (2001) *Widening Participation in Post-Compulsory Education,* London: Continuum Studies in Higher Education.

Thompson J. and Bekhradnia, B. (2010) *Male and female participation and progression in Higher Education: further analysis,* Higher Education Policy Institute.

Tobin, L. (2011) 'Rise of the stay-at-home students' in *The Guardian* (12/08/11).

Trout, P. (1997) 'Disengaged students and the decline of academic standards' in *Academic Questions* (Spring 1997).

Truscott, B. (1945) *Redbrick and These Vital Days,* London: Faber and Faber.

Tuchman, G. (2009) *Wannabe U: Inside the Corporate University,* University of Chicago Press.

US DofE (2006) *A Test of Leadership: Charting the future of U.S. Higher Education, A Report of the Commission Appointed by Secretary of Education Margaret Spellings,* Education Publications Center.

Vasager, J. and Shepherd, J. (2011) 'David Willetts Opens up Market for Student Places' in *The Guardian* (28/06/11).

Vedder, R. (2011) 'Forgive Student Loans: it's the second worst idea ever' in *National Review Online:* http://www.nationalreview.com/articles/279716/forgive-student-loans-richard-vedder [accessed 28/07/12].

Weimer, D. L., and Vining, A. R. (1992) *Policy Analysis: Concepts and Practice,* New Jersey: Prentice Hall.

Weinberg, S. (2004) *The Higher Education Act: Possible Implications for Accountability and the Assessment of Student Achievement,* NYU Faculty Resource Network, available at: http://www.nyu.edu/frn/publications/approaching.assessment/higher.education.act.html [accessed 28/07/12].

Wignall, A. (2007) 'How to fulfil those great expectations' in *The Guardian,* (20/02/07).

—(2006) 'You have passed Go. Pay £3000', in *The Guardian (26/09/06).*

Willetts, D. (2011a) *Universities and Social Mobility,* Sir Ron Dearing Lecture, Nottingham University (17/02/11).

—(2011b) *Speech to UUK Spring Conference 2011,* Woburn House: London (25/02/11).

—(2011c) *Speech to The Guardian HE Summit,* America Square Conference Centre, London (16/03/11).

Williams, J. (2008) 'Constructing social inclusion through further education – the dangers of instrumentalism', in Journal *of Further and Higher Education,* 32 (2), 151–160.

—(2010) 'The student customer is not always right' in *Spiked Online,* http://www.spiked-online.com/index.php/site/article/9847/ [accessed 28/07/12].

—(2011a) 'Constructing Consumption: Deconstructing Subjectivity' in Molesworth, Nixon and Scullion (eds) *The Marketisation of Higher Education and the Student as Consumer,* Oxon: Routledge.

—(2011b) 'Raising Expectations or Constructing Victims? Problems with promoting social inclusion through lifelong learning', in *International Journal of Lifelong Education,* 30 (4).

Winch, C. (2000) *Education, Work and Social Capital,* London: Routledge.

—(2002) 'The Economic Aims of Education' in *Journal of Philosophy of Education,* 36 (1).

Wolf, A. (2002) *Does Education Matter?* London: Penguin.
Woolcock, N. and Malvern, J. (2008) 'We pay the fees so you supply the mod-cons, students tell universities', in *The Times* (17/11/08).
Young, M. (1971) *Knowledge and Control: New Directions for the Sociology of Education,* Buckingham: Open University Press.
Zernike, K. (2010) 'Making College 'Relevant'' in *The New York Times* (3/1/10).
Zhu, Y. and Walker, I. (2011) Paper Presented at Royal Economic Society Conference, (18/4/11).

INDEX